Foreign Affairs
The World At War

Foreign Affairs November 2016

TABLE OF CONTENTS

Introduction   1
Gideon Rose

THE CLOUDS GATHER

July 1933
Hitler's Reich [Excerpt]   3
The First Phase
Hamilton Fish Armstrong

April 1935
The Expansion of Japanese Rule   6
Edgar Packard Dean

January 1937
The Jews of Eastern Europe [Excerpt]   10
Desider Kiss

April 1938
America Rearms [Excerpt]   12
Hanson W. Baldwin

January 1939
Armistice at Munich [Excerpt]   14
Hamilton Fish Armstrong

THE STORM BREAKS

October 1939
Hitler Could Not Stop [Excerpt]   20
Hermann Rauschning

January 1940
Blitzkreig [Excerpt]   25
Henry J. Reilly

October 1940
The Downfall of France [Excerpt]   28
Hamilton Fish Armstrong

October 1941
Anglo-American Pitfalls [Excerpt] 30
Geoffrey Crowther

October 1941
Let Japan Choose [Excerpt] 32
Eugene Staley

Winter 1991/92
Pearl Harbor: Documents: The Rising Sun in the Pacific 36
Samuel Eliot Morison

April 1942
America at War: Three Bad Months [Excerpt] 39
Hanson W. Baldwin

July 1942
Hitler's Transfers of Population in Eastern Europe [Excerpt] 47
Hedwig Wachenheim

October 1942
The Spirit of Resistance [Excerpt] 50
Victor Vinde

January 1943
America at War: The First Year [Excerpt] 56
Hanson W Baldwin

October 1943
Datum Point 59
Hamilton Fish Armstrong

January 1944
America at War: The End of the Second Year [Excerpt] 68
Hanson W. Baldwin

THE WINDS BLOW

July/August 2013
The Road to D-Day [Excerpt] 74
Rick Atkinson

October 1944
America at War: The End Begins [Excerpt] 88
Hanson W. Baldwin

July 1945
America at War: Victory in Europe [Excerpt] 91
Hanson W. Baldwin

October 1945
America at War: Victory in the Pacific [Excerpt] 100
Hanson W. Baldwin

January 1946
America at War: The Triumph of the Machine [Excerpt] 110
Hanson W. Baldwin

January/February 1995
The Atomic Bombings Reconsidered 114
Barton J. Bernstein

AFTER THE STORM

October 1947
Political Problems of a Coalition [Excerpt] 127
William L. Langer

November/December 2003
That Was Then: Allen W. Dulles on the Occupation of Germany [Excerpt] 138
Allen W. Dulles

January 1947
The Nuremberg Trial: Landmark in Law [Excerpt] 143
Henry L. Stimson

July 1947
The Sources of Soviet Conduct [Excerpt] 146
"X" (George F. Kennan)

October 1948
The Atom Bomb as Policy Maker [Excerpt] 149
Bernard Brodie

April 1949
The Illusion of World Government [Excerpt] 151
Reinhold Niebuhr

May/June 1996
The Myth of Post-Cold War Chaos [Excerpt] 154
G. John Ikenberry

November 14, 2016

Introduction

Gideon Rose

The attack on Pearl Harbor.

Foreign Affairs and its parent organization, the Council on Foreign Relations, were founded in the early 1920s by veterans of the Woodrow Wilson administration's diplomatic and military efforts. Shocked by the country's turn to isolationism in the wake of the Great War, they followed with increasing dread the world's march toward yet another conflict during the 1930s. The pages of the magazine tracked the rise of Adolf Hitler and the Nazis, the growing conquests of imperial Japan, the stirrings of military preparedness in Washington, and ultimately the most devastating conflagration the globe has ever seen.

Seventy-five years after the United States entered that war, we offer this collection to showcase all that remarkable coverage, giving today's readers a taste of how things looked to knowledgeable observers watching events in real time. As I combed through our archives, I was struck by just how well informed close readers of the magazine would have been about what was going on, why, and what needed to be done about it.

Who knew, for example, that Foreign Affairs was running articles about the state of eastern European Jewry in 1937? Or that we published a fascinating portrait of how the French public gradually turned against the Nazi occupation? Or that the basic contours of the war's long, complex military operations were understood and predicted so early and accurately? From Herbert Rauschning, Reinhold Niebuhr, and George Kennan to Henry Stimson, Allen Dulles, and Bernard Brodie, from William Langer and Samuel Eliot Morison to Rick Atkinson and Barton Bernstein, the authors included here constitute a galaxy of talent, and the result is both insightful and gripping.

From the mid-1930s to the late 1940s, world history changed course dramatically. At the start of the period, a few unprepared democracies tripped over themselves as they tried to resist the rise of aggressive dictatorships around the world. By its end, the United States was leading those democracies in the establishment of a fundamentally new and liberal world order that would provide unprecedented peace, prosperity, and freedom for billions of people for generations to come. This book tells the story from start to finish, with all the drama and turbulence in between; we hope you enjoy reading it as much as we enjoyed putting it together.

© Foreign Affairs

July 1933

Hitler's Reich [Excerpt]

The First Phase

Hamilton Fish Armstrong

Hitler with his staff at his "Wolf's Lair" field headquarters in 1940.

A people has disappeared. Almost every German whose name the world knew as a master of government or business in the Republic of the past fourteen years is gone. There are exceptions; but the waves are swiftly cutting the sand from beneath them, and day by day, one by one, these last specimens of another age, another folk, topple over into the Nazi sea. So completely has the Republic been wiped out that the Nazis find it difficult to believe that it ever existed, at any rate as more than a bad dream from which they were awakened by the sound of their own shouts of command, their own marching feet....

Not merely is he wiped out, but the memory of him is wiped out. It is pretended that he never was. His name is not mentioned, even in scorn. If one asks about him, a vague answer is given: "Oh yes – but is he still alive? Maybe he is abroad. Or is he in a nursing home?" This does not merely apply to Jews and Communists, fled or imprisoned or detained "for their own protection" in barbed-wire concentration camps. It applies to men like Otto Braun, leader of the great Social Democratic Party, perennial Premier of Prussia.... It applies to the series of Chancellors furnished by the once-powerful Center Party.... The generals who were talked about as embryo dictators – von Seeckt, Groener, even the powerful von Schleicher – are no more heard of or seen.... Stresemann is not merely dead, but has been dead as long as the last Pharaoh. The men who ruled Germany in these fourteen years have been swept away, out of sight, out of mind, out (according to the program of Dr. Goebbels, propagandist-in-chief) of history....

The Stahlhelm, the organization of front-line veterans, credited with having saved the country from anarchy and communism in several post-war crises, but feared by the Nazis as a possible rival to their S.A., has been broken and subjected....

The Reichswehr, on which General von Schleicher counted and which as recently as last December could and would have supported him in a determined move to establish authority in the name of the flickering Republic, now stands glumly aside.... All that its leaders can do is wait (as the Royal Italian Army has waited without result) to see whether there will ever come a moment of chaos when they might step in to reëstablish the state they were enlisted to serve. It is a forlorn hope.

One by one continue to fall the last possible citadels of defense against uncontradicted Nazi dictatorship.

Federal Germany is gone. The Gleichschaltung law disposes of the prerogatives of the separate States, and Nazi leaders have been named Statthalter, with power from Berlin to dismiss State governments should they not prove fully amenable. Eminent Lutheran and Reformist theologians are hastily forming a new and unified Reichskirche to meet the fear of the Nazis that opposition or weakness might develop in the former 28 autonomous churches in the various States, and to simplify their drive against religious organizations which are not two parts blood and iron and only one part milk of human kindness. The Socialist trade unions ... were finally seized outright on May 2, the day after the celebration of the "Festival of National Labor." Their buildings were occupied by storm troops, their officers were jailed, and their funds were appropriated to the new Nazi union which is now organizing all labor as an instrument of party will....

The judiciary has been weeded over with minute care, and as a result many judges ... have either resigned or been dismissed. Henceforth, says a circular of the Prussian Ministry of Justice, judges will be tested for their patriotism and social principles and will be put through periods of service in military camps to school them in "martial sports." In Nazi eyes the conception of abstract justice is outworn. The essential justice is that which serves the higher ends of the state.

Even the great Nationalist Party, co-partner with the Nazis in the March election which followed the fall of von Schleicher, and supported by all the clans of Junkers, monarchists, landed proprietors, former army officers and officials, is left hanging in the air, its toes barely touching the ground, slowly strangling in the noose of its own devising. When on the night of January 30 von Papen persuaded Hitler to join him in making the election, he thought that he had prepared the way for his own conservative forces to swallow up the Nazis. But it was the reverse which happened....

These new rulers of this new people have also a new vocabulary. In literature and art, in the professions and even in sport, new specifications replace taste and skill and experience.... A work of art or a performance of any sort is not good unless the creator is an Aryan, preferably Teutonic to the last drop of his blood (if such a being exists), preferably a Nazi, and in any case not a liberal or a Jew. Music, the theatre, the cinema, all have been bent to Nazi propaganda aims. The universities are being "cleansed." ... The press has also been "assimilated," unfriendly or lukewarm or liberal or pacifist or "internationalist" or Jewish proprietors, editors and correspondents have been expelled, and Nazi commissars put at the side of the writers who remain. Attention is centered almost exclusively upon news of the revolution – texts of proclamations, speeches of leaders, accounts of mass meetings and celebrations...

The German Republic was a puny plant. Beneath the inch or so of top-soil in which its seeds were hastily placed were a dozen unyielding strata, packed down and solidified by tradition and usage. The servitudes of a punitive peace treaty, the galling preponderance of France and her allies in Europe, the economic distress following the defeat and the inflation, all these hindered its growth. The cultivators, from Ebert and Scheidemann through Stresemann and Brüning down at last to von Papen and von Schleicher, cared less and less about saving it.... But the final determining condition which caused the Republic's death was that it had no nourishment from below. As an eminent German said to the writer two or three years ago: "We made a republic; but there were no republicans." [Full Article]

HAMILTON FISH ARMSTRONG, *Editor of* Foreign Affairs.

© Foreign Affairs

April 1935

The Expansion of Japanese Rule

Edgar Packard Dean

Samurai members of the First Japanese Embassy to Europe (1862); Shibata Sadataro, head of the mission staff, seated; and Fukuzawa Yukichi to his right.

WITHIN the recollection of men still alive, Japan has evolved from a small feudal principality voluntarily shut off from the rest of the world to the status of a Great Power whose influence is felt in every quarter of the globe. Seventy years ago Japan had a population of 33 million. The present Japanese Empire, excluding Manchuria, has 92 million subjects, a total surpassed only by the United States, the British Empire, Russia and China.

The Consolidation of Japan Proper. At the time of the Meiji Restoration in 1868 Japan consisted of the four large islands of Hokkaido, Honshu, Shikoku, and Kyushu, and a peripheral zone of 4,068 islets. The total land area was 146,689 square miles. The country was economically self-sufficient; and the population, some 30 million, had been stationary for a century and a half.

The first instances of expansion should be regarded as the realization of nominal claims of sovereignty. In 1875 the Kuriles, a chain of thirty islands lying to the northeast, were formally annexed (see map). The islands had and still have a primitive economy, furs and fish being the principal exports. Two years later Japan acquired the Bonin Islands after a period of contested ownership with the United States. These are a group of 27 islands, with a population of 5,000 souls; they have a vegetation of tropical luxuriance and possess many valuable woods. (The adjoining Volcano Islands were annexed in 1891.) In 1879 the LuChus were annexed by virtue of Japan's position as feudal overlord. The LuChus form an archipelago of 55 islands. The soil is fertile, and crops are fairly diversified, sugar cane being the most important. The people are of the same racial stock as the Japanese.

Formosa (Taiwan) was acquired from China in 1895 as a result of the Sino-Japanese War. This is a tropical island situated a hundred miles off the Asiatic coast, with a land area of 13,840 square miles. It is Japan's tropical storehouse par excellence. Tea, rice, lumber and sugar are produced in abundance, sugar being considered the most important for the future development of the island. Camphor woods are extensive and the world output of camphor is virtually controlled by Japan. Formosa and the neighboring Pescadores have a population (1932) of 4.6 million, of which 94 percent are Chinese. The Japanese, though only 5 percent of the total population, control the island's political and economic life.

Korea (Chosen). Economic preponderance in the independent kingdom of Korea (85,613 square miles) was granted to Japan in 1905 as a result of the Russo-Japanese War. Formal annexation came in 1910. Korea is mainly agricultural, the chief crops being wheat, barley, rice and the soya bean. In 1910 the population was 13.3 million; in 1932 it was 20.5 million, of whom only 2.5 percent were Japanese. Here, too, the Japanese colonists dominate the political and economic life.

Sakhalin. By the Treaty of Portsmouth in 1905 Russia gave all the island south of the fiftieth parallel to Japan. The Japanese part, Karafuto, has a land area of 14,000 square miles. The island has a cold, foggy climate with only one hundred days suitable for crops. Fisheries, forests and mines constitute the basis of the economic life. Small but rich coal deposits are being actively developed. Of a total population of 295,000, nearly 98 percent are Japanese.

The Expansion of Japanese Rule

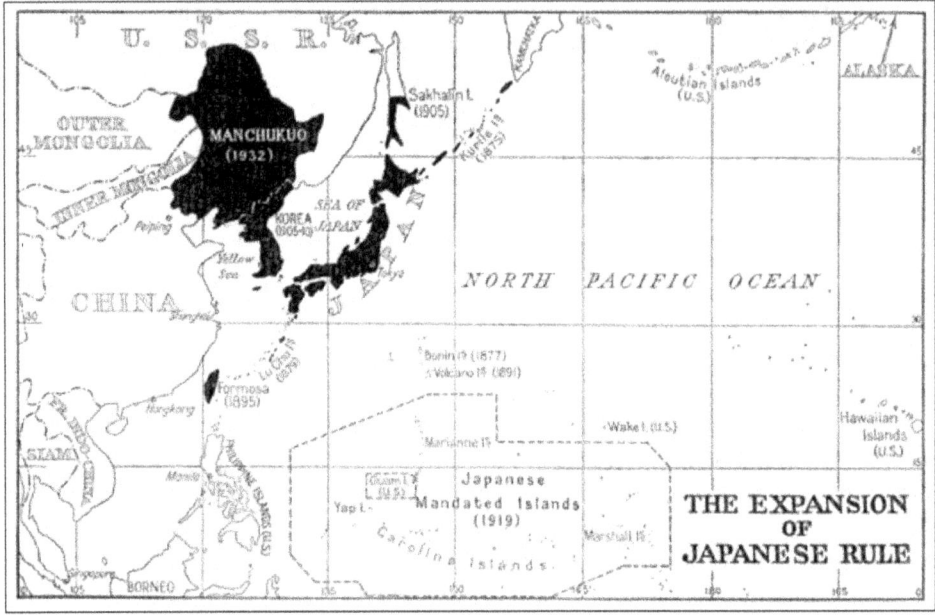

The Mandated Islands. One of Japan's few gains at Versailles was a mandate over the formerly German-owned islands in the Pacific comprising the Marianne, Caroline, and Marshall groups. The Mandated Islands are a salient dividing the United States possession of the Hawaiians in the east from the Philippines in the west, and making Guam an isolated American colony in a Japanese sea. The Mariannes have a fertile soil adapted to the raising of sugar cane, and Japan has done much to promote this crop. The Carolines, with valuable phosphate mines, are the administrative and naval center for the entire mandated zone. The Marshalls are rich in coconut palms and copra. The three archipelagoes as a group are highly valuable to Japan. They are valuable for strategic reasons, for their products, and as an outlet for Japanese emigration. As a result of government policy, the population of the islands has increased from 52,000 in 1920 to 80,500 in 1933. Of this gain of 28,500 all but 1,500 were emigrants from Japan. It is these Mandated Islands that Japan has been accused of fortifying in violation of the Treaty of Versailles.

Manchukuo (including the Kwantung Leased Territory and the South Manchuria Railway Zone). Territorially this is the largest of the areas controlled by Japan. It comprises some 548,000 square miles, an area more than twice the size of Texas, and has a population of 31 million, of whom 2.7 percent are Japanese. Of all the areas under Japanese control, Manchukuo is by far the most valuable. The soil is fertile and gives Japan a supply of many food products. The amount of cotton which is raised can be increased, though never to the point of supplying the mother country with all its needs. There are extensive mines of coal and iron, key minerals in which Japan is very deficient. As an outlet for population and as a source of raw materials, Manchukuo is invaluable to overcrowded, industrialized Japan.

This brief sketch of the growth of the Japanese Empire reveals several significant facts. In the first place, the expansion of the Empire was not an affair of logic. It had begun even before Japan was mistress of her own household. Expansion into the Pacific and over the Asiatic continent was simultaneous, forcing Japan to become both a naval and a land power. In the second place, many of the Japanese gains have been made at the expense of China, and this despite the fact that the two Powers have been formally at war for only a few months in a sixty-year period. Thirdly, the number of Japanese in the colonies is not large. Only 5 percent of the population of Formosa is Japanese; in Korea the proportion is only 2.5 percent; and in Manchukuo 2.7 percent.

Lastly – and this is a strategic consideration – the Japanese possessions are so situated as to form two cordons of defense against any approach to Eastern Asia by sea. The inner defense lies along the line of the islands of Japan proper, extending northeast to the Kuriles and southwest to Formosa. The outer cordon is a great arc, beginning on the Japanese mainland behind Tokyo, reaching east and south to the Bonin Islands, passing through Yap, and terminating south of the Philippines. Inside these two strategic lines, Tokyo can exercise its naval strength as it chooses. Japan is, indeed, free to become a continental power because she is already a Pacific power.

EDGAR PACKARD DEAN, of the Research Staff of the Council on Foreign Relations

© Foreign Affairs

January 1937

The Jews of Eastern Europe [Excerpt]

Desider Kiss

A water carrier in the Lublin Ghetto, Poland

OF THE ten and a half million Jews who live in Europe some nine million are to be found in the eastern half of the continent, in the cities and on the plains between the River Inn and the Ural Mountains. During the last four years the policies of the Nazi dictatorship in Germany have cast a shadow over the lives of all these Jewish millions. So far they have been unwilling to believe that anti-Semitism in the starkly brutal form which it has assumed in Germany will spread abroad. Yet the fact remains that a great and highly civilized European nation has excommunicated half a million people merely because they adhere to the Jewish religion or belong to the so-called Jewish "race," and thus has given other lands a dangerous example of positive anti-Semitism.

...

Except in Russia ... the situation today of the Jews of Eastern Europe must be painted in sombre colors. Almost everywhere the liberal and humane ideals of the nineteenth century are under attack, and as they weaken the anti-Jewish trend becomes more pronounced. The Jew is being pressed back with varying degrees of violence into his mediæval state of servitude. The most tragic victim of this social process is the assimilated, cultivated Jew. The orthodox masses of Galicia, Bessarabia and Ruthenia are less conscious of what is happening except when there is some special outbreak of terror. They still live the religious, often mystic, life of their ancestors – a life of fear and privation, cut off from contact with the world around them, confident in Jehovah's wisdom and relying on his protection. The waves of anti-Semitism now rising in Eastern Europe are as incapable of destroying these Jewish masses as were the systematic persecutions they underwent in past centuries. [Full Article]

DESIDER KISS, Foreign Editor of the Pester Lloyd of Budapest

© Foreign Affairs

April 1938

America Rearms [Excerpt]

Hanson W. Baldwin

American factories churned out weapons of war such as these Consolidated Vultee Aircraft Corporation B-24 Liberator bombers.

THE passage of the Neutrality Act in 1936 and the strong support recently given in Congress to the Ludlow Resolution (providing that war can be declared only if approved by a national referendum) are merely two manifestations of the great strength not only of American isolationists but of that considerable body of public opinion which is determined to have peace at almost any price.

But as the United States has sought to withdraw more and more into its shell it has felt the urge to make that shell strong. The pending Army and Navy annual supply bills tentatively call for the expenditure in 1939 of about $980,326,812, an increase of more than $50,000,000 over the national defense budget for 1938. That already constitutes one of the greatest peacetime armaments budgets in American history. On top of this, on January 28 the President urged Congress to authorize a largescale, long-range expansion of the Navy and a further modernization of the Army at a total estimated cost of $1,300,000,000 over and above the regular annual defense budget.

These apparently contradictory trends – the one pacifist and the other militarist – are not so incongruous as they might appear on the surface; they represent in fact a reversion to that old policy enunciated earlier in the century by another Roosevelt – "speak softly and carry a big stick." In the first postwar decade when the nations were toying with disarmament the big stick was whittled down considerably. Our national defense policy followed the familiar pattern of our history, except that in addition to the usual disarmament "by neglect" we were practising disarmament by precept and by treaty.

But those days are done and the time for a really big stick has come again. Ever since President Roosevelt took office in 1933, the Army, the Navy and their air forces have been steadily increasing in size and power. Today, under the impetus of the world armament race, the process is being accelerated at an even faster tempo.

… It is, of course, impossible to know in advance what use we might have to make of our Army and Navy, other than to defend the territory of the United States – continental and insular. According to the Vinson Bill now before Congress the Navy must be "adequate" to protect both the Atlantic and Pacific coasts, our insular possessions, "our commerce and citizens abroad," and to "support our national policies." In reality, however, neither the Army nor the Navy is at present being prepared to implement any such far-reaching policy. Presumably we have no aggressive designs in any quarter of the world. But what about our existing interests in the Far East and in South America – will we under any circumstances fight to protect them? If so, shall we find it necessary or expedient to undertake joint operations with other Powers in defense of common interests? If so, in what areas and to what extent? Or is it rather our intention to strengthen the Army and Navy to the point where they can singlehanded enforce any policy the American Government believes to be worth fighting for, without needing or accepting outside help? These questions – and the many others which they suggest – cannot, of course, be answered here. But we must keep in mind that they exist; otherwise any discussion of the proposed Army and Navy expansion programs is quite unrealistic.

The Army and Navy are at present prepared to defend both coasts of the United States against simultaneous invasion, and at the same time to protect Hawaii, Panama, Alaska and probably South America from any attacks that can reasonably be foreseen. But they cannot – either with our existing defense establishments or with any now contemplated – defend the Philippines or Guam; they cannot keep the Open Door in China from being slammed in our face; and they cannot protect our commerce and citizens everywhere. The question before the American people, therefore is: Shall the Army and Navy be strengthened sufficiently to enable them to do any one, or all, of those things? [Full Article]

HANSON W. BALDWIN, Military and Naval Correspondent of the New York Times; author of "The Caissons Roll"

© Foreign Affairs

January 1939

Armistice at Munich [Excerpt]

Hamilton Fish Armstrong

GERMAN FEDERAL ARCHIVE

Chamberlain, Daladier, Hitler, Mussolini, and Ciano pictured before signing the Munich Agreement, which gave the Sudetenland to Germany.

FUTURE historians, distributing praise and blame for the Munich "settlement," will of course take into account the long chain of things done which ought not to have been done, and of things left undone which ought to have been done, that winds itself through all the last twenty years of European history. In the light of this inheritance some of them will conclude that the policy which Chamberlain began unfolding early in 1938 was inevitable, and that Daladier and Bonnet too were inevitably forced, first to recognize that they could not balk that policy, then to adopt it with all the fervor of the convert. Others will think that with foresight and determination British and French statesmen could even in 1938 have maintained a balance of power on the Continent.

We cannot discuss here the more remote links in the chain. We cannot discuss who was responsible for errors in the Treaty of Versailles; for the League's inability to meet the heavy tasks laid upon it; for the deterioration of the world's economy; for the French and British failure to make a better effort to achieve disarmament; for Britain's subsequent neglect to rearm effectively through a long period when cabinet members were frequently assuring Parliament that all necessary steps were being taken; for delays in reforming the French social structure; for the failure of French aëroplane production from 1936 to 1938; and for all the other mistakes of commission and omission (on both sides of the Atlantic) during the past twenty years.

Our task is to make a chronological examination of the Czech-German crisis of 1938. We shall try to set down, before all the details are known, but on the other hand while what we do know is still vividly in our minds, just one single chapter of the story which future historians will have to write in full. We shall see how what started as a two-sided negotiation between the Czech Government and the German minority in Czechoslovakia became an international negotiation under the auspices of an English "mediator," Lord Runciman. And we shall see how the mediation ended in a series of international ultimata – from Hitler via Henlein to Beneš, then from Hitler to Chamberlain, then from Chamberlain and Daladier to Beneš, and finally from Chamberlain, Daladier, Hitler and Mussolini to Beneš.

It is not for an American to say that Englishmen or Frenchmen should fight and die for causes which do not seem to them vital. The moral issue, then, will be touched on in these pages only incidentally. But this country has been profoundly affected by the destruction of the balance of power in Europe. So great a shift portends, if it does not register, a shift in the balance of power in the world. The results for the United States – economic, political and strategic – in both of the bordering oceans and in Latin America, are incalculable. So also are the results for international law, the observance of treaties and the concept of sovereignty in a world of which the United States, much as it wishes the contrary, is more and more inexorably shown to be a part. We are entitled, then, and indeed are in duty bound, to examine the political conceptions and the day-by-day actions which gradually led Britain and France to Munich. It is the expediency of those actions that concerns us here. Ethical aspects will be touched on only incidentally, and then, I hope, not in a moralizing vein; for I have too much fault to find with much of our own foreign policy from 1919 onwards to feel the inclination to utter any moral reproach.... Was Munich "peace for our time"? Appeasement if it means anything means satisfaction. Is Germany satisfied with her acquisition of a territory roughly the size of Belgium, close on the heels of her acquisition of Austria? Is her ally Italy satisfied? Viewing the present state of mind in those two countries, are the British and French people satisfied? Can we say that the Europe we survey at the close of 1938 is satisfactory all-around and that there is promise of sincere reconciliation, orderly evolution and peace?

The Munich honeymooners ran rapidly into some inclement weather.

Within a few days of the signing of the Munich Agreement and the Anglo-German pact the German Minister of Economics, Walther Funk, was touring the Danubian and Balkan States, cashing in economically on Germany's new pivotal position in Europe. Back in Berlin from Ankara, Sofia and Belgrade, he reported on October 17 that he had "great economic reconstruction plans" for Jugoslavia, Bulgaria and Turkey, where there would be "extensive road construction and telephone and cable installation," and outlets also for German railway and bridge material and the products of Germany's machine and chemical industries. In return, he continued, "Southeastern Europe and Asia Minor possess almost everything Germany needs, especially ores," and he noted that they also could supply Germany with agricultural products. He had made a trade credit of 150,000,000 marks to Turkey. On October 18, still striking while the iron was hot, he extended another of about 60,000,000 marks to Poland. On October 25 the results of his visit to Belgrade materialized in a new German-Jugoslav trade treaty, planned to balance exports and imports and to fix a stable ratio between the mark and the dinar.

Obviously, it is too early to speak of complete German economic dominance in the Balkans as a foregone conclusion. Rumania, Jugoslavia, Bulgaria, even Hungary, have a good deal of will and some ability to resist. But the trend is plain. Mr. Chamberlain hastened to accept as natural Dr. Funk's erection of a German commercial juggernaut in Central and Southeastern Europe. For geographic reasons, he remarked on November 1, Germany must be considered as occupying "a dominating position" in that region. But there were men both in the City and in business who were less well satisfied. And across the Channel, some Frenchmen thought indignantly of the billions of francs spent since the war on arming France's protégés so that they might continue an independent political and economic existence, and of the sums devoted in those lands to propaganda on behalf of French trade and culture.

… British opinion, divided as to the effectiveness of Mr. Chamberlain's course in trying to pacify the dictators by kind words, concessions and pacts, united in annoyance when Chancellor Hitler, eagerly seconded by the controlled German press, began referring to all of Mr. Chamberlain's critics as war-mongers. The Fuehrer's speech at Saarbruecken on October 9 contained two extraordinary statements. The first was that "at the beginning of this year" he had "made a decision to lead back into the Reich 10,000,000 Germans who still stood outside." That remark branded as false all the Fuehrer's own statements made subsequent to January 1938 to the effect that he would respect the integrity and independence of Austria and Czechoslovakia. The other was a warning that the present leadership in England and France must not be changed if satisfactory relations with Germany were to continue. "In England," said Hitler, "it is merely necessary that instead of Chamberlain, a Duff Cooper or an Eden or a Churchill come into power. We know that the aim of these men would be to start war." The subsequent press campaign recalled the Italian vendetta of February against Mr. Eden. But this affair was even more aggravating. Direct instruction from the head of the German Reich as to who should or should not participate in the British Government was received in London with very poor grace.

On the heels of this came reports [l] that Germany, in return for holding to the ratio embodied in the Anglo-German naval treaty, was preparing to demand a 3-to-1 preponderance in the air. Hadn't the Anglo-German pact of September 30 referred to the naval treaty as symbolic of the desire of the two peoples never to go to war again? Would Hitler so soon call it into question by attempting to trade it off for concessions in the air? The reports were not verified, but they persisted and added to the restlessness of some sections of the British public. Nor was the sense of exacerbation diminished by fresh pressure in the German press for prompt attention to Germany's colonial demands, summed up in the October 29 statement of General von Epp, leader of the German Colonial League, that what was wanted was not a colony here and there but Germany's former colonial realm "as a whole."

In the Far East, too, Munich had repercussions. Seizing on Britain's moment of obvious weakness, the Japanese on October 12 landed troops in South China and attacked Canton, isolating the British Crown Colony of Hong Kong and cutting off China's last direct link with the sea. As a result, Hong Kong besides facing bankruptcy has become a liability strategically. In July both Chamberlain and Halifax had given Japan blunt warnings that British interests in China would be protected. Now all that happened when Japanese troops began operating outside Hong Kong was a "reminder" from the British Ambassador in Tokyo that Anglo-Japanese relations might be disturbed.[li] The Far Eastern ally of Germany and Italy had chosen her moment well. The success enabled the Japanese extremists to settle themselves more firmly than ever in the saddle. Their next step was to slam shut the door in China which western Powers had liked to think was still ajar.

Then with a crash burst the campaign of anti-Jewish atrocities, unleashed throughout Germany at a given hour one night in retaliation for the assassination in Paris of a German diplomat by a seventeen-year-old Jewish boy who had seen his family pauperized and shunted from pillar to post by the Nazis. Horror and disgust swept in a wave across the civilized world. Nowhere was the reaction more instantaneous and sincere than in England. Even Hitler's best friends were surprised and shocked by the pogrom and by the official decrees which followed the mob violence. The Marquess of Londonderry, inveterate apologist for German actions and ambitions, denounced as "detestable" what Hitler had ordered or permitted to occur in his rigidly controlled state.[lii] He still was for peace through the establishment of personal contact between the leaders of the Four Great Powers; but he was plainly on the defensive, and stated clearly that if Britain ever were "faced with a policy of truculence and threats," and could not overcome it by the policy she had tried to follow, namely peace based on friendship and a "helping hand," then she would adopt another policy in return, namely one of truculence and vehement protestation. And Lord Baldwin, who thought on October 4 that "there was nothing else on earth" that his successor Mr. Chamberlain could have done in September except go to Berchtesgaden, expressed on December 8 what his feelings had been when "like a bolt from the blue" he found "world misery" at "our very doors." He appealed for funds to help relieve the explosion in Germany of "man's inhumanity to man" – to help find for thousands of men, women and children "despoiled of their goods, driven from their homes" some "hiding place from the wind, a covert from the tempest." The German press replied elegantly by calling him some of the names they had called President Benes.

In France less concern was evident, at least in the press, over the latest wave of Jewish atrocities. Traditional French hospitality to political and racial refugees, though severely strained by previous influxes of unfortunates, and dampened somewhat by the Government's quite frank desire not to offend the Reich, nevertheless still survived. There probably was no less worry in France than in England over the post-Munich international outlook. But social questions engaged public attention; and the general relief that peace had been preserved, and the abstinence of great sections of the French press from any really critical appraisal of the results of the Daladier Government's foreign policy, for a time held anxiety in check. As in England, the sponsors of the Munich Agreement kept up a good front. M. Bonnet, addressing an enthusiastic assemblage of his constituents at Perigueux on October 8, sought to allay French regrets over what had happened to Czechoslovakia. "One criticism I cannot accept," he said, "and that is that France broke her word. That is not true. We never swerved from our attitude. We said: 'If Germany resorts to force, France will carry out her pledges of assistance.' We also said we would seek by every means to avoid such a resort to force and to obtain a peaceful solution of the Sudeten German problem" (Temps, October 10). On October 27 M. Daladier, breaking with the more leftist sections of the former Popular Front, maintained a similar thesis: "I cannot permit anyone to speak of the capitulation of France.... What was done at Munich was a rational act."

On both sides of the Channel rearmament meanwhile continued, and on both sides of the Rhine....

...What judgment is one to give, in such circumstances, on the policy of appeasement? An American, be it repeated, must try to avoid moralizing. But must he accept the policy as having been expedient? The American Ambassador at the Court of St. James' seems to do so. Urging that differences between democratic and dictator governments be not allowed to grow into "unrelenting" antagonisms, he remarked on October 19 that "after all, we have to live in the same world whether we like it or not." Observers not so close to 10 Downing Street see difficulties in a live-and-let-live policy in a world where others do not reciprocate good feelings and soft actions. Might not Mr. Chamberlain have done better to adopt a motto implying more reciprocity than "appeasement"? After all, one can feel that by September 29 something like the Munich Agreement had become the only alternative to open hostilities without feeling that the policy which pointed toward Munich necessarily was expedient in February, or in July, or in August, or when Chamberlain decided to "come across" to meet Hitler face-to-face at Berchtesgaden, or in the days immediately thereafter, or even in the more doubtful period after Godesberg. Would a bolder choice of the sort of a world in which Englishmen have traditionally shown that they do positively like to live, rather than acquiescence in the idea that they must live in a different sort of world "whether they like it or not," have won the former and staved off the latter? The possibility is suggestive for Americans who see some such eventual choice before them too.

Certain general disadvantages in the Chamberlain method which Mr. Kennedy's phrase unconsciously indicated have become even plainer since he spoke. How will what was done to Czechoslovakia at Munich affect the sanctity of international contracts, not as moral instruments but as the incarnation of a rule of law? What sort of engagements will European states henceforth consider as possessing any particular value? What, further, becomes of the idea of sovereignty? The principle of self-determination, taken into account by the authors of the Treaty of Versailles along with historical, economic and strategic factors, often is in conflict with the concept of national sovereignty. What consequences will the recent application of the principle of self-determination have for nations like England and France, which can establish no possible ethnic claim to ownership over their far-flung possessions?

There has been no fighting – at least over Czechoslovakia, though of course in Spain and China undeclared international war has been raging as bloodily as if it had been punctiliously announced. For the avoidance of bloodshed over Czechoslovakia the peoples of Europe give thanks, and Americans with them. Furthermore, so long as a war has not actually begun it always may in some manner be avoided altogether. But viewed from the western side of the Atlantic the situation today prevailing in Europe does not seem to be so much peace as an armistice. Even Mr. Chamberlain must feel like saying with the Psalmist, "I labor for peace, but when I speak unto them thereof they make them ready to battle." ... [Full Article]

HAMILTON FISH ARMSTRONG, *Editor of* Foreign Affairs

© Foreign Affairs

October 1939

Hitler Could Not Stop [Excerpt]

Hermann Rauschning

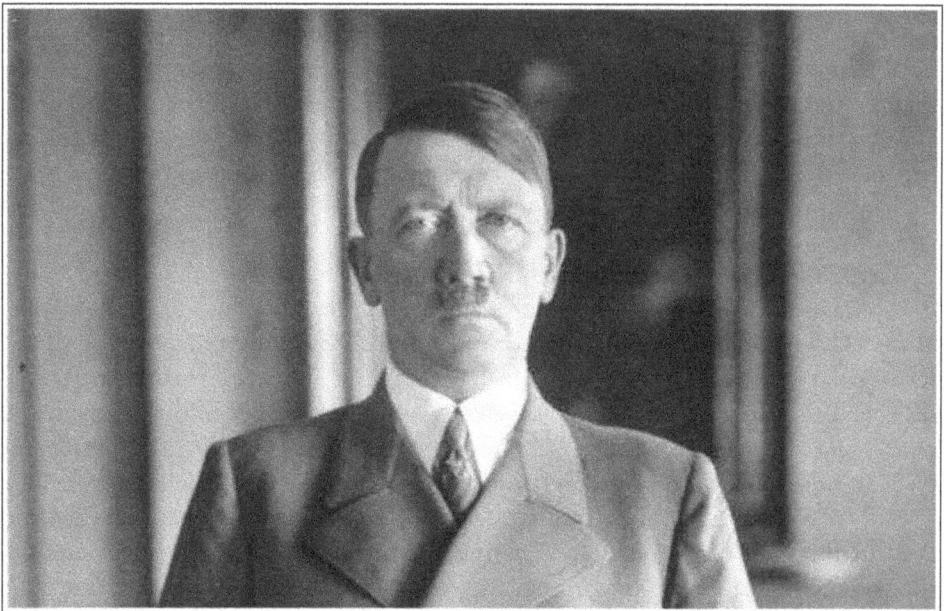

Hitler in 1938

SOME people believed that Hitler could be induced by certain limited concessions, made dependent on his fulfillment of certain specified conditions, to change his methods of procedure and limit his aims. Germany would then cease to figure as a troublemaker in the world and would fit into a new international equilibrium. The view was based on a number of sound assumptions and was justified by the example of the movement for German unification between 1864 and 1870. Bismarck often expressed the idea. He said that once the unified Reich had been constituted, one of his main concerns would be to create general confidence in its pacific intentions. After rectifying the injuria temporum (the Bismarckian phrase), German policy would set itself the task of becoming a force for peace in Europe. Bismarck's national policy was based exclusively on force and was eminently "practical." But its objectives were always limited. At the given moment it saw the necessity of fixing its own limits, and never overstepped them.

Sharply in contrast with Bismarck's "art of the possible" stands the hazy, impulsive policy of William II. At a critical moment during the latter's reign, the Morocco crisis of 1905, Sir Arthur Nicolson remarked that the German Foreign Office did not itself know what it wanted; and he went on to say that the real danger in German policy was not so much its expansionist outlook as its vagueness. That was entirely true. It was impossible to work out a policy of harmonious collaboration with a person who did not know what he wanted. William II based his foreign policy on surprises and sudden impulses, and that fact, much more than Germany's striving for world power, led directly to the World War.

Hitler's policy at first differed strikingly from the policy of William II. It differed also from the policy of the Weimar Republic, which was also – though for different reasons, chiefly the Republic's inherent weakness – wavering and uncertain. Hitler's policy was outspoken and showed that it was clearly conscious of its goals. Frankly nationalistic, setting out to revise the Versailles Treaty and rectify an obvious injuria temporum, it moved along lines noticeably similar to Bismarck's. It began, then, as the continuation of a policy which, in the previous century, after achieving its aims, resulted in over forty years of peace for Europe.

In the beginning Hitler's policy was strictly and exclusively national. Its one aim seemed to be to transform the "little Germany" that Bismarck had founded into the "greater Germany" that still lived in the thoughts of all German patriots. This was to be achieved by revision of the territorial provisions in the peace treaty, which in the long run would have proved unendurable anyway. Germany possessed many friends among her sometime war opponents. These would probably have approved of such a reasonable policy if certain revolutionary features attending its application, along with its terroristic methods, had not chilled good will abroad and intensified foreign hesitations. Even so, however, one still could argue that the extravagant features of the new German policy were superficial and would automatically correct themselves in due course.

Objectively, however, the policy of the Third Reich could be considered constructive only so long as it had a definite and limited scope. In other words, only if National Socialist foreign policy aimed specifically at uniting actually German territories in an enlarged German state could it expect that other states would tolerate the gradual reorganization of Europe under German leadership.

During the early years of the National Socialist régime, therefore, foreign criticism took the form mainly of moralistic disapproval of certain of its domestic methods. There was little disapproval of its aims as such. Indeed, some authoritative interpreters abroad exerted themselves to put even the domestic procedures of National Socialism in a better light, thereby strengthening a natural inclination on the part of many persons to ignore certain repulsive revolutionary aspects of the movement as being strictly the private concern of the German people, explicable probably on the basis of the delight which they habitually take in discipline and "order." The austere forms which the German national regimentation adopted were calculated in many ways to beguile foreign criticism. The advantages of authoritarian methods became apparent in the ease with which Germany overcame many surface symptoms of her social and economic crisis. The country seemed to be on the road to order and recovery; hence (it was assumed), once a transitional period of unrest had passed, on the road to peace.

The domestic opponents of National Socialism among the former ruling classes of Germany reached a similar view. During a first short period they grossly underestimated the strength of the new régime. There followed a second short period when the dominant feeling was one of shock and resentment at its brutal methods. Then finally the educated and patriotic middle classes settled down in the persuasion that the various outrages of National Socialism were ephemeral revolutionary manifestations that must needs be borne with for the time being.

In non-Nazi circles in those days, among the army leaders, the bureaucracy and in business, the word was passed to allow the revolutionary outburst "to wear itself out." The movement, it was said, would "clean itself up." The wise course was felt to be to enter the Party so as gradually to reshape it from within. Many important holders of public office felt, of course, that it was impossible to reconcile the Party's unscrupulous conduct with their individual consciences and that it was their duty to resign. They were reminded that to do so would only strengthen the new movement and intensify its extremist character. They were told that rather it was their duty to hold their positions as long as possible, in order gradually to weed out the "catastrophe makers," or, at the worst, to serve as brakes on " the plunge into catastrophe." Reasoning of this sort had a certain semblance of soundness, and it appealed, among others, to men such as Baron von Neurath, in foreign affairs, to Count Schwerin-Krosigk, in finance, and to Eltz Rübenach, in commerce. They decided not to break with National Socialism, but to work with it, to retard and moderate it, and to prevent another lapse into bloody revolution.

These motives were intelligible enough, but they were none the less mistaken. The National Socialist movement could not be reformed. It was obeying an inner ironbound law of its own being. It was following the relentless urge toward extremism to which every revolutionary movement is destined. The collaboration of conservative and competent officials and men of affairs strengthened the régime; but they could not change it. They wore themselves out, and the movement went on regardless. An adjustment of the nature of a civil war was avoided; but in the end the price was the total capitulation of the "restorative" elements in the ruling and educated classes and of the liberal and democratic elements in business and labor.

The question now arises whether, in following a sometimes temporizing and sometimes frankly pro-Nazi policy, the western democracies did not make the same mistake in the foreign field which inside the Reich led to the capitulation and enslavement of the German citizenry as a whole. The policy of domestic collaboration avoided civil war within Germany; the conduct of the democracies in compromising with Germany aimed to avoid a European war. To be sure, there would be solid grounds for reasoning the other way round – that the disposition of the democracies to yield, without setting any clearly discernible limits on what they would yield, was what first made war a real danger. However that may be, there can be no doubt that pressure upon Germany from abroad might very well have led to the fall of the National Socialist régime. But would that have led to any lasting adjustment for Europe as a whole? Perhaps the overthrow of National Socialism would have set a genuinely revolutionary development in motion. A period of anarchy might then have ensued. Or a strictly Prussian and militaristic solution might have been found, compared with which even the National Socialist régime might have seemed the lesser evil.

How such a gross misreading of National Socialism could have held sway for so long in the world is hard indeed to comprehend. The lack of critical sense and foresight shown by German business leaders doubtless contributed. They merely noticed with satisfaction the temporary relief brought them through currency control and the new methods of dealing with labor problems, and they paid no attention to the disturbing revolutionary disintegration of all the elements composing what is called public order. They were simply obsessed by the idea that National Socialism's energetic methods offered the chance of at least temporarily escaping from the general world depression....

... "Lebensraum," the space required by a nation for living, is not, in Nazi terminology, the mere space sufficient for subsistence under a system of free exchange of goods. It means a domain sufficiently comprehensive to provide Germany with "absolute" freedom of action. The limits of that domain expands automatically as the requirements of modern warfare expand. What would have been adequate in the year 1880 to make Germany self-sufficient and "sovereign" had become wholly inadequate by the end of the World War. To become truly "sovereign" under postwar conditions Germany must now expand the domain under her control eastward as far as the Caucasus and including the Ukraine, and westward as far as the open sea. She must have the oil of the Caucasus, the minerals of the Ukraine, and the grain of Hungary and Rumania; also she must have the steel of northern France, control of the shore line of Belgium, Holland and northern France, and the colonial domains at present belonging to those countries. In this policy the law of the minimum controls; for the soundness of the policy varies with that factor, not with the maximum.

Such are the ideas of National Socialism. The fundamental thing which emerges is the impossibility that olive branches and concessions in this or that particular could ever serve any purpose. Either it is "full sovereignty" for Germany or it is nothing.

Hitler's foreign policy therefore allowed him no freedom of choice. His particular aims all stood in a fixed and necessary relation to his comprehensive aim: "full sovereignty" for Germany as a "world people." Germany will be satisfied only when she controls a completely self-sufficient territory. In the perspective of that policy, all projects for a return to a purely economic organization of the world necessarily remained uninteresting. The dependence of parts of the world on the whole, and the interdependence of all the parts, are the very things which must be rectified, abolished, and this not on doctrinaire grounds but because of the plain requirements of practical politics. Thus there were but two alternatives: Germany's complete surrender, her renunciation of all hope of becoming a "world people;" or an uncompromising struggle to attain the complete goal. The goal can be attained only by German control over all Europe. Only when European hegemony has been won can National Socialism accept a system of international exchange of commodities as not any longer disturbing to German sovereignty. In view of this, the effort to make National Socialist imperialism believe that it would do well to go back to a system of free international exchange, and to explain to National Socialist chieftains that other countries are only too anxious to help them satisfy Germany's economic needs, were perfectly fatuous....

... Any régime that has limited aims can compromise, can dispense with the complete attainment of every one of its objectives. Not so National Socialism. Compromise, for National Socialism, is death. The alternatives facing it were and are total success or total capitulation. One or the other. Any retreat abroad would at once create difficulties at home that would lead to the régime's collapse. From it, then, one could and can expect nothing but an unwavering advance along the road on which it set out – the road to hegemony over Europe and to world revolution. [Full Article]

HERMANN RAUSCHNING, former Nazi President of the Senate of the Free City of Danzig; author of "The Revolution of Nihilism"

© Foreign Affairs

January 1940

Blitzkrieg [Excerpt]

Henry J. Reilly

The Ju 87 "Stuka" dive-bomber was used in blitzkrieg operations

"BLITZKRIEG" or lightning war is not a German term for just any kind of quickly waged and violent war. It is a name for a special kind of quickly waged and violent war which has a technique of its own. The ideas which lie back of this technique began taking shape in Germany in the period after the failure of either the Allies or the Germans to break through on the Western Front during 1915 and 1916, and they matured after the outbreak of the civil war in Spain.

While some of the guiding conceptions of the Blitzkrieg were tried out in Ethiopia, the results were not considered conclusive. The Ethiopians were a semi-savage people, and they lacked the modern armament and equipment necessary to offer the Italian invaders the kind of resistance essential if Blitzkrieg were to receive a real and complete battlefield test. But Spain furnished a fine proving ground. Then Albania was a dress rehearsal. And in Poland the system was put to the final proof.

Blitzkrieg [Excerpt]

The technique of Blitzkrieg is based on the principle of surprise as opposed to an effort to crush an enemy by bringing an overwhelming superiority in numbers and armament to bear against him. It can be likened to the swift and deadly thrust of a rapier as opposed to the crushing blow of a battle-axe or a war club. The objective is not the enemy civilian population but the enemy armed forces, both ground and air....

... The suppression of the Polish Republic proved that a brave, well-armed, well-equipped and well-trained army, according to ordinary standards, is incapable of resisting a Blitzkrieg attack. True, the Poles made strategic errors in trying to defend all of Poland, instead of accepting the invasion of the western part of their territory as a necessary evil and concentrating their army where it could have made the most effective resistance. But even if they had adopted this correct strategical procedure they would have been beaten. The reason for this statement is that the Poles lacked the aviation, the well-armored tanks with cannon, and the large-caliber anti-tank and anti-aircraft guns which would be needed to stop and defeat a Blitzkrieg force. And I might say in passing that the Regular Army and National Guard of the United States would fare no better today, and for exactly the same reason.

The Blitzkrieg technique, as exemplified so successfully in Poland, follows certain well-defined successive steps:

1. An airplane attack is made on all enemy aviation and aërodromes.

2. An airplane attack is made on all railway junctions and stations, barracks, depots, bridges, and motor convoys on roads – that is, everything used by an army for mobilization and concentration. (If the aviation is large enough it carries out 1 and 2 simultaneously.)

3. While this is going on, the artillery of all calibers which already is in place near the border heavily shells all the enemy batteries, trenches and other works, while the regular infantry assaults and takes them. Heavy bombing and light diving bombing and machine gunning by airplanes assist this preparation. These operations by the troops armed and trained for hard combat open the way for the Blitzkrieg troops. Of course, if there are no minor fortifications or organized resistance of any kind at the frontier, this step is not necessary. In those circumstances the Blitzkrieg troops start their invasion directly after steps 1 and 2 have been executed.

4. The light divisions made up of motorcycle infantry and machine guns, armored cars, light tanks (carried in trucks), horse cavalry, and sometimes horse artillery (light) and artillery carried in trucks, lead the way.

5. After the light divisions come the armored divisions, each composed of about 400 tanks (generally medium-sized), motorized infantry, artillery, anti-tank and anti-aircraft artillery, and engineers. The light and armored divisions are closely supported

by aviation, which is ready at all times with heavy bombing planes and diving light bombing and machine gun planes to help overcome any enemy resistance.

6. Next come infantry and artillery in motor trucks. Italy also has arrangements to pick up infantry units and fly them wherever needed. Reliable reports indicate that Germany has at least four regularly organized air regiments, each consisting of a fully equipped and armed regiment of infantry, with the transport planes necessary to fly them all at one and the same time. The purpose of these is to reinforce quickly the light and armored divisions should they meet with more resistance than they can overcome with their aviation support. The troops would not be landed by parachute in the rear of the enemy, a procedure few military men would care to sanction; troops so landed would probably be a present to the enemy. Instead, the airplanes land just out of enemy artillery range, in the rear of their own troops.

The Blitzkrieg troops do not attempt to engage in knockdown, drag-out combat with enemy troops prepared for this type of fighting. Instead, they go around the flanks, leaving the other job to the regular divisions which come plodding along in the rear.

No nation in Central Europe or the Balkans is armed and equipped, any more than was Poland, to withstand a Blitzkrieg attack. Nor is Turkey. The possibility therefore is that in the not distant future either Germany or Italy, or both, will use their special light and armored divisions and aviation to enforce their will in these regions should any of the countries involved dare to be intractable either economically or militarily. [Full Article]

HENRY J. REILLY, D.S.M., Colonel of Infantry in the U. S. Army in the World War, now Brigadier General in the Officers Reserve Corps; former editor of the Army and Navy Journal; war correspondent for various American publications in many campaigns

© Foreign Affairs

October 1940

The Downfall of France [Excerpt]

Hamilton Fish Armstrong

Adolf Hitler strolling in front of the Eiffel Tower in Paris, 23 June 1940.

ON May 10 Hitler sent his troops into Holland, Belgium and Luxembourg. He chose the moment well. For although there had been repeated alarms of just such a German invasion, the British and French Governments were neither of them in a condition to react to the actual event instantly and in unison. In both countries there was a cabinet crisis.

On April 9 Hitler had occupied Denmark and invaded Norway. In the month that had intervened since then the German invaders had not secured complete success. The British expeditionary force hung on in Narvik. But the larger bodies of British troops landed at several points on the Norwegian coast, and the French and Polish troops that had accompanied or followed them, had been forced to retire. The British people, press and Parliament were busy on May 7, 8 and 9 debating the responsibilities for what seemed more and more clearly to have been a great Allied failure. So intense was the domestic political dispute that on May 10, despite the dangers of the military situation created overnight by Germany's invasion of the Low Countries, Neville Chamberlain felt obliged to resign as Prime Minister and the King asked Winston Churchill to form a new Government.

In France there also was a cabinet crisis over Norway, though it had not come openly to a head. Premier Paul Reynaud had become worried by the conduct of French operations there, and had decided that General Gamelin, the French Commander-in-Chief, ought to be replaced. This added new intensity to M. Reynaud's long-standing feud with M. Daladier, for General Gamelin was Daladier's man. The row had come to such a pitch by May 9 that when M. Reynaud brought the matter up in a Cabinet meeting that afternoon M. Daladier threatened to resign if General Gamelin were replaced; and M. Reynaud was ready to resign if General Gamelin were not replaced. After their sharp discussion, the Cabinet members separated for the night feeling that there would have to be a show-down and probably a new Cabinet the next morning.

But before the new morning dawned Hitler had struck. The French Cabinet closed ranks temporarily, for obviously there could not be a change in the High Command in the very moment of attack. But General Gamelin can hardly have felt sure that morning whether or not he was to remain Commander-in-Chief. Perhaps, even, the uncertainty of his position was one of the factors which impelled him to make rather rash decisions about how many troops should be sent into Belgium and Holland, and about how far they should be ordered to try to go. That is speculation. But the fact of bickering and discussion in the French Cabinet over the efficiency of the French High Command at the very moment when the campaign opened in the Low Countries is not in doubt. And this French Cabinet crisis joined with the Cabinet crisis in England to provide the Germans, not with the opportunity for a tactical surprise, for that was hardly conceivable, but with an opportunity to act when the men in charge of the destinies of both the Allied Powers were preoccupied with personal and political quarrels.... [Full Article]

HAMILTON FISH ARMSTRONG, *Editor of* Foreign Affairs

© Foreign Affairs

October 1941

Anglo-American Pitfalls [Excerpt]

Geoffrey Crowther

Roosevelt and Churchill aboard HMS Prince of Wales.

IF the Declaration of the Atlantic, signed by the President of the United States and by the Prime Minister of the United Kingdom and released to the world on August 14, 1941, is taken merely as a restatement of the democratic faith in international relationships, nine-tenths of its significance will be lost. The ideas are not particularly new nor is the language unduly inspired. Its true significance lies in the identity of the signatories and in the place where it was signed. The Declaration marks, in effect, the assumption by the two great English-speaking democracies of the leadership of the free world. It serves notice that, when the victory has been won, the ideas that will be dominant in the world will be the faiths and the aspirations and the doctrines that are common to Britain and America. The fact that its only date line is "The Atlantic Ocean" is as significant as the signatories. Nothing could have more dramatically demonstrated the change that has come over the rôle of the Atlantic in the popular thinking of both countries. The ocean is no longer a barrier, a moat, a gap in space. It is a highway, a meeting-place, a common avenue of approach. Implicit in every line of the Declaration is the proclamation that hope for the world's future – the only hope – lies in the continued collaboration of the Oceanic Commonwealth of Free Nations.

To the overwhelming majority of Englishmen, and to very many thousands of Americans, this recognition by both nations of their common needs and common responsibilities is the great good that is coming out of the evil of the war, just as for their fathers (and the thought is a warning) the League of Nations was the offset that could be made against the misery of the last war. It is an inspiring picture – two great nations, each satisfied with what it has got, and therefore devoid of any aggressive intention, joining together to police the world on behalf of their joint ideals of personal freedom, social security, and liberated commerce. To adopt this as a deliberate policy, as the heads of the two Governments have now done, has required, or will require, very substantial changes in the ideas that have prevailed and in the attitudes that have been adopted hitherto. Nor are these changes required on the American side alone. It is true that the American people, if they are to sail this new course, will have to modify or abandon two of their hitherto most cherished beliefs – the first that they need not concern themselves with what goes on beyond the oceans, and the second, that there is a natural and historical antipathy between American and British interests. But the British people too will have to change both their beliefs and their policies. Britain, it is true, has always been a naval power, but her diplomacy has nevertheless always looked inwards to Europe. With the sole exception of 1870, there has not been for centuries past a European crisis without Britain's participation from the start as one of the protagonists. Indeed, Great Britain has usually been the organizer of whatever Grand Alliance is current. If Britain's policy is now to be based on her membership of an Oceanic Commonwealth, she will not find it so easy (and perhaps not so necessary) to form her European coalitions. This is a point of view which the British Dominions have always expressed; it now receives enormously stronger backing. The shifts in traditional policies will thus need to be as great in the one country as in the other. In the psychological field, it is in Britain that the adjustment to the new policy will probably be found most difficult. If the American people have to learn the responsibilities of their strength, the British people have to learn the limitations of their weakness – and there can be little doubt which of the two is the more painful adjustment to make.... [Full Article]

GEOFFREY CROWTHER, Editor of the Economist, London

© Foreign Affairs

October 1941

Let Japan Choose [Excerpt]

Eugene Staley

Scroll depicting the Great Fire of Meireki

JAPAN is, to put it bluntly, out on a limb. It is possible for the United States, acting in concert with the British nations, China, the Dutch Government of the East Indies, and the Soviet Government of Siberia, to saw off that limb; or, alternatively, to help Japan to descend from her precarious perch, on fair terms, with a minimum of injury and loss of face. We should be prepared to do the first and offer to do the second. Then let Japan choose....

... Japan's one chance – and many intelligent Japanese must be reflecting along this line – is to enter negotiations for a general settlement with the anti-Axis governments and to do it now while she still has some bargaining power. We, on our side, while prepared to meet any aggressive Japanese moves by force, should also be willing to offer Japan terms of settlement which take account of the legitimate aspirations of the Japanese people, particularly their need for assurance of economic opportunities abroad in the form of market outlets and raw material supplies.

A two-part program will be outlined below. It is suggested that the United States, acting with the British nations, China, the Netherlands East Indies, and the Soviet

Union, should adopt such a program as its policy in the Pacific. The first part of the program consists of pressure on Japan. The second opens a gate for Japan to pass through peacefully – a way out which is compatible both with the legitimate, long-run interests of the Japanese people and with the interests of other peoples in the Pacific.

The program of pressure on Japan would include: (1) continued and increased aid to China, in order to immobilize as many Japanese troops as possible in the Chinese theater of war; (2) close collaboration with the British and the Dutch in continuing to build up the already strong defenses of Manila, Singapore and the Netherlands East Indies, plus aid in strengthening the Soviet forces in Eastern Siberia in any way feasible; (3) economic blockade of Japan, or the threat of it, to be enforced by total non-intercourse between members of the coalition and Japan, by refusal of fuel and other facilities to Japanese ships anywhere in the world, and by inducements and pressures calculated to persuade all the other countries with which Japan might hope to trade (mainly the Latin-American countries) to follow similar policies.

The consequences for Japan of the economic isolation which such a coalition would be able to enforce without the moving of a single warship or plane into Japanese-controlled waters would be devastating. The effects would not be immediate, but they would be inexorable. Japan is peculiarly dependent upon uninterrupted economic relations with areas outside the range of her own naval power for the materials necessary to sustain her military efforts and to maintain the living standards and the employment of her people. This is the result of her geographical situation and the nature of her economic life.

The Japanese islands are very densely populated. The inhabitants are accustomed to a moderate standard of living, but a rising one. This has been brought up to its present level, despite a rapid increase in population, by the creation of a highly-specialized, modern, industrial system of production. Japanese productivity, and hence the capacity of Japan to provision its people and its military forces, is nowadays geared to machine tools, factories, railways, ocean shipping, and the like. This structure rests, in turn, upon raw materials which are not available in adequate quantities and varieties in Japan proper, or in the territories so far conquered by Japan. If Japan were subjected to a total economic blockade the area to which she would have access contains insignificant or very inadequate sources of petroleum, nickel, mercury, platinum, magnesite, mica and asbestos. Serious deficiencies would be felt in iron, copper, aluminum, manganese, lead, zinc, and the ferro-alloys such as tungsten and molybdenum. Moreover, Japanese facilities for turning out machine tools, specialized precision instruments, automotive products, aircraft and many other strategically important items are inadequate. There would be a greak lack of wool, fertilizers, lumber, wood pulp, and vegetable fibers. Furthermore, quite aside from the havoc wrought by shortages of such fundamental raw materials, Japanese industry and the Japanese political and social system would come under a terrific strain in adjusting themselves to the loss of overseas markets. These have provided income and employment for millions of Japanese producers of such articles as raw silk, textiles and miscellaneous small manufactures, as well as for many shipping workers.

Japan is known to have stocks of oil and other strategic materials on hand which would probably last for a good many months. She would find it possible, moreover, to make many adaptations and adjustments in view of the emergency. The fact remains that she is extremely vulnerable to pressures of an economic character, and that these can be applied against her at a long distance from her own sphere of political and military influence. This is the central reason why today one is able to characterize Japan's position as one of weakness.

Japan is also weak in other ways. Suppose her leaders decide to fight rather than yield. Suppose they set out to break the economic blockade by military force. Where can they attack? Japan has a large and modern navy. But the needs of a modern battle fleet for fuel and repairs restrict its field of operations to a limited radius from its own or friendly naval bases. This means that the Japanese Navy can exercise dominant power in its home waters. But it also means – and this is a crucial point – that unless and until new bases are conquered much farther afield, Japan is not in a position to launch any serious attack against the real centers of power of the coalition which would be arrayed against her. The best Japan can do is to attack their outposts in eastern or southeastern Asia. But while she was doing this she would continue to suffer from the attrition of the long-distance economic blockade. She would use up precious supplies. She would expose her navy and merchant marine to the risk of serious losses. And her own vital centers of power would be exposed to attack by long-range bombers, particularly if Siberia is available as a base for such attacks. The latter threat is not something the Japanese can ignore. Japanese industries and transportation lines are relatively concentrated, and great sections of Japanese cities – almost literally "made of wood and paper" – are highly inflammable. The distance from Vladivostok to Tokyo, Osaka and Yokohama is some six hundred miles – roughly the same as from English airfields to Berlin.

There is a further point which Japanese military leaders must take into consideration. If they choose the desperate gamble and try to break the economic blockade by force there is no assurance either that the places attacked can actually be captured without crippling losses, or that once a new piece of territory has been captured they will actually be able to get out of it the resources that Japan needs, and to get them out quickly enough to stave off utter exhaustion at home. Meantime, there would be the problem of maintaining communication lines against flank attacks by the strong Powers with which Japan would be at war....

... Suppose Japan decides to break the blockade towards the south. The Philippines are now strongly enough defended so that Japan could seize them only by a major effort and at the risk of considerable losses. Once conquered, the Philippines would make an important contribution to the Japanese economy in iron ore and vegetable fibers and in a few other respects. But this would merely begin to ease the pressures of the economic blockade.

Farther south are the islands of the Netherlands East Indies, rich in raw materials. The islands themselves have a not inconsiderable defense force, including planes and small naval units. But the greatest bulwark of their defense is the heavily garrisoned naval base at Singapore. It would be risky for the Japanese to launch an attack in this area without having first reduced Hong Kong and the Philippines, so that the defenses of these places, too, help to protect the Netherlands Indies. Finally, if Japan did succeed in conquering the Netherlands Indies or important parts of them without having suffered a major disaster, her problems would still not be solved. Oil wells and refineries would probably be blown up, and it would take a considerable time to get production going again – especially since much of the necessary technical equipment would not be available to Japan. Sea communications might be under constant harassing attack....

... With our adoption of the firm front described earlier in this article should go a sensible and fair appreciation of Japan's needs and the offer of a plan of settlement which will give her a way out – not just a "face-saving" way out, but a real and lasting solution of her basic problems. The Japanese people, crowded on a few islands though they are, can maintain and increase their living standards if they are able to engage in large-scale processing of raw materials. These, as already noted, must come in considerable part from abroad. And the Japanese must be able to sell abroad a substantial proportion of their produce, thus earning foreign exchange with which to pay for imports. Unless they can do this they cannot live – at least, not at an acceptable standard of consumption. If conditions for the Japanese people are not "livable" there can be no long-run stability in the Pacific. This is a fact well recognized by American students of the Far East and by American officials. Upon this fact our offer to Japan should be based. Such an offer ought to lessen the likelihood that Japan will choose a contest of force. If Japan does choose force, our offer would provide a basis on which the war might more quickly be brought to an end in the very probable event that the Japanese people found their situation becoming progressively hopeless.

... No one can say for sure whether an offer of settlement on some such basis as this would stand any chance of success.... [Full Article]

EUGENE STALEY, Professor of International Economic Relations, Fletcher School of Law and Diplomacy; author of "Raw Materials in Peace and War," "World Economy in Transition" and other works

© Foreign Affairs

Pearl Harbor: Documents: The Rising Sun in the Pacific

Samuel Eliot Morison

Attack on Pearl Harbor.

On 6 December President Roosevelt played his last card for peace-a personal message to Emperor Hirohito, begging him for the sake of humanity to withdraw the military and naval forces from southern Indochina which threatened the Philippines, Malaya, Thailand and "the hundreds of islands of the East Indies." Hirohito did not want war with the United States, but he wanted still less to lose his throne. Showa Restoration would have been turned into Showa Deposition if he had refused to go along with Tojo at this point. So he said nothing.

On Sunday morning, 7 December 1941-the "day that will live in infamy"-the Japanese ambassadors, as instructed by their government, asked for an interview with Mr. Hull at 1300 in order to read Tojo's reply to the proposals of 26 November. That time had been selected because it was just twenty minutes before the scheduled hours (0750 Honolulu time) of the attack on Pearl Harbor. Owing, it seems, to a delay by the embassy staff in deciphering and translating this note, the interview was postponed until 1400. Mr. Hull had already been handed a copy of Admiral Kimmel's message, "Air attack on Pearl Harbor. This is not a drill," but he thought it might be a mistake; and having no official word of war he believed he should hear what Nomura and Kurusu had to say. So he received them at 1420.

It was now 0900 December 7 in Hawaii. The first sad and bloody hour was over. The burned and shattered bodies of more than a thousand Americans lay strewn along airfields, on charred decks, or trapped beneath the waters of Pearl Harbor.

The Japanese attack on Pearl Harbor was but a part, and in their estimate not the most important part, of a comprehensive plan for the Greater East Asia War. Formulated bit by bit, this plan was finally brought together at a Supreme War Council on 6 September 1941. Not Pearl, but pearls of greater price were the objective: populous islands fabulously rich in natural resources and strategic materials, possession of which would enable the Japanese to dominate East Asia and, finally, the world. As Admiral Yamamoto put it in his "Top Secret Operation Order No. 1" issued to the Combined Fleet on 1 November 1941, Japan intended "to drive Britain and America from Greater East Asia, and to hasten the settlement of the China Incident.... When Britain and America have been driven from the Netherlands Indies and the Philippines, an independent, self-supporting economic entity will be firmly established. The vast and far-reaching fundamental principle, the goal of our nation-Hakko Ichiu-will be demonstrated to the world."

The comprehensive war plan was this: first, without a declaration of war, to invade Thailand [Thailand had been infiltrated and the government suborned in advance; it issued an order to its troops to cease firing about three hours after the attack began on 8 December], destroy the United States Pacific Fleet and deliver air strikes on the Malay Peninsula and Luzon. After the initial surprise, to effect conquest of the Philippines, Borneo, British Malaya (including Singapore) and Sumatra. When these were secure, Japanese amphibious forces would converge on the richest prize, Java, and mop up the rest of the Dutch islands. Intensive development of Netherlands East Indies resources would begin at once, and to secure these new possessions a "ribbon defense" or defensive perimeter would be established, running from the Kurile Islands through Wake, the Marshalls and around the southern and western edges of the Malay Barrier to the Burmese-Indian border.

Although the Japanese knew that America had ample resources to stage a comeback, they expected that, with Australia and New Zealand isolated, and the Japanese

Navy operating from interior lines, any attempt of the British and American Navies to break through the defensive perimeter could be beaten back for eighteen months or two years. By that time, it was hoped, the English-speaking powers would be so stricken by fighting a two-ocean war as to be ready to make peace on the basis of Japan's retaining most of her conquests. She could then proceed at leisure to complete subjugation of China. Over half the world's population would then be under the economic, political and military control of the Son of Heaven. If not eight corners of the world, five at least would be under "one roof as Emperor Jimmu once predicted.

No such vast plan of quick conquest had ever been formulated in modern history. Apparently it never occurred to the average Japanese that there was anything morally wrong with it. Japan's divine mission to realize Hakko Ichiu was taken for granted, and so all means to that end were proper. Surprise attacks, regardless of plighted word, were part of Bushido, the code of the warrior. The earlier wars of Japan on Russia and China had begun that way and both had been successful; Heaven obviously approved.

The place of the Pearl Harbor attack in this comprehensive scheme was purely and simply to eliminate the United States Pacific Fleet so that it could not interfere with the numerous amphibious operations necessary to conquer the "Southern Strategic Area." It was "a strategic necessity," said Admiral Nagano.

Up to about 1940 the Japanese planned in the event of war with the United States to keep their Combined Fleet in home waters. The high command either knew or guessed correctly that the United States naval plan was to fight its way across the Pacific via the Marshalls and Carolines, taking Truk en route, in order to relieve the Philippines. The Japanese proposed to make this voyage very unpleasant for the United States Fleet, by submarine attacks and land-based or tender-based air attacks mounted from sundry airfields and lagoons in the Marshalls and Carolines. Whatever ships survived would be pounced upon by an overwhelmingly superior Combined Fleet in the Philippine Sea, and there annihilated. That was sound strategy; fortunately for us, the Japanese abandoned it for something more spectacular and less effective.

1 Excerpted from History of United States Naval Operations in World War II, Vol. III. Reprinted by permission of Little, Brown and Company.

© Foreign Affairs

America at War: Three Bad Months [Excerpt]

Hanson W. Baldwin

REUTERS

THE history of our first three months at war must be painted in somber colors. The United States Navy suffered the worst losses in its history. Guam and Wake were captured by Japan. In quick succession the enemy overran most of the Philippines, seized Hong Kong, swept over Singapore, principal bastion and base of the United Nations in the Far East, and reduced various strategic points in the Netherlands East Indies one by one. As these lines were written, the surging tide of conquest was nearing Rangoon, entry port for the Burma Road, and was imperiling India. Southward it was menacing Australia. In the West, the Anglo-American "life line" to Britain and Iceland had been safeguarded and strengthened; but Germany had commenced long-range submarine raiding operations in our coastal waters. All over the world, ship sinkings were increasing to totals which approximated those of the war's worst months, and freight storage yards at American seacoast cities were clogged with products of the

"Arsenal of Democracy" awaiting merchant shipping which could transport them to the fighting fronts.

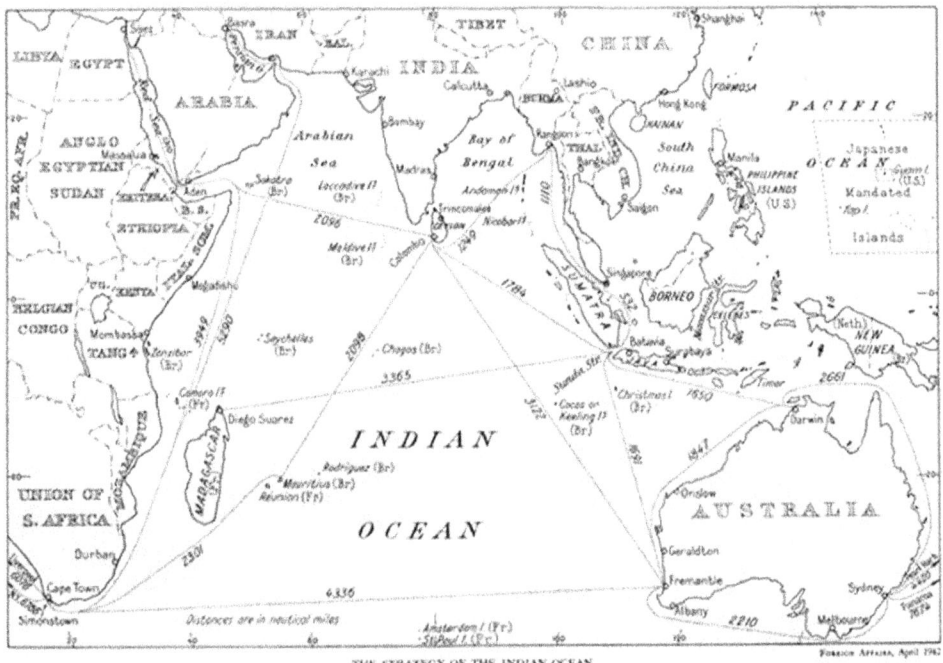

THE STRATEGY OF THE INDIAN OCEAN

Thus in less than 90 days the strategic picture of the war had been considerably altered. The United Nations had suffered their worst defeats since the fall of France. As spring approached, the short-range prospects were grim. From the long-range viewpoint, however, the basic factors which have been the strength as well as the weakness of the United States have not in every case been modified by the events of its first three months of participation in a shooting war. We still possess many advantages.

Until December 7, 1941, the military struggle which had been in progress could be described in the truest sense as a battle for the domination of Europe. For more than two years the headlines had been telling of its progress. The Nazi legions had swept across country after country, raising the swastika from the North Cape to the Acropolis. Even the battles in Africa had been, strategically speaking, part of the struggle for the Old World; and the German invasion of Russia came as one of its final chapters. But already the war quite evidently was "growing out" of Europe. Only the unexpectedly stout Russian resistance, which prevented the Germans last autumn from reaching the Caucasus and erupting into Asia Minor, and the lease-lend aid given to Britain by the "nonbelligerent" United States, held Hitler within the bounds of Europe. A turning point of some sort thus was at hand even before Pearl Harbor. The military war which had been raging for two years across Europe was about to break the bounds of the Continent, just as the political war, the economic war, the ideological war, had long before become one for the world much more than for a continent.

The Japanese attack on Pearl Harbor did not merely add to the list of belligerents. It enlarged the theater of military operations from a continent to the world. Today, though a number of nations still are ostensibly neutral, there really are no non-belligerents. This has become the greatest war in history, the first to deserve absolutely the term "World War." In one sense it is a war of hemispheres, waged over the continents and the seven seas. In the fullest sense it is total war; it touches all fields, all values, of human interest.

In this war of the world the United States occupies strategically and geographically a central position. It lies behind two great oceans, between a Europe which is virtually dominated by Hitler and an Asia of which the eastern portion is dominated by Japan. We dominate the western shores of the Atlantic and the eastern shores of the Pacific. But the opposing coasts, thousands of miles away, are in the hands of our enemies. Russia also occupies a central position between two enemies, the European Axis states and Japan. But Russia is a great sprawling land mass, in the midst of a continent, with few and precarious gateways to the warm seas and without adequate communications with the other United Nations.

Our strategic position is, in the main, fairly clear. A glance at a world map shows that in defense of our continental territory and of the Western Hemisphere as a whole the United States occupies the inestimable advantage of the "interior position." So long as our forces remain in the Western Hemisphere they can be moved over shorter distances and by shorter lines of communication than any enemy force which can be brought into play against them. We are operating, as it were, from the center of a circle and can rush our forces quickly to any threatened point on the circumference. The Axis, on the other hand, in order to attack us must come great distances over the seas, moving their forces around the perimeter of the circle.

The advantage of the "interior position" is very considerable in war. The Germans have found it a material factor in producing their European victories. If the day comes when we are fighting with our backs to the wall, it will be important to us also. Under present circumstances it is useless. For defensive actions cannot win wars. The "Maginot Line mind" and the military theories that helped to give rise to it have been proved fallacious. We can say that in general the Third French Republic died because it was obsessed by the doctrine of the timid defensive. Wars can be won only by carrying the fighting to the enemy, by the offensive. In total wars what is demanded is theoffensive à outrance. This is particularly true in this war. There can be no victory for us if Germany retains control of most of Europe, if Japan creates her "Greater East Asia Co-prosperity Sphere" and holds China's coasts in fief and exploits Malaya's tin and rubber and the rich supplies of the Indian archipelago. We cannot hope to alter either situation by defensive operations. Only conquest can counter and redeem conquest. If Germany and Japan are to be defeated, if the world is to resume something like its former political shape, the United Nations, and particularly the United States, by far the most powerful of the partners, must reconquer Europe and Asia. The war must be carried to the enemy.

Once we accept this as an axiom of victory, we must also accept some of the disadvantages that geography has imposed upon us. For in the European theater and in the theater of the Western Pacific and Asia our enemies have the advantage of the interior position, and it is we who must operate over great distances around the perimeter of continents and archipelagoes. To carry the fighting to our enemies, to win the war, we must transport troops, planes, men and supplies in amphibian operations of unprecedented magnitude across thousands of miles of the Atlantic and Pacific. And no matter where we choose to strike, it is Japan in the Far East and Germany in Europe who will be able to move their forces the most quickly and over the shorter distances. This is one continuing strategic disadvantage which we must recognize, accept and overcome if we are to win this war.

Yet we still have a great advantage. The United Nations possessed, and still possess, territories and bases in the Western Pacific-Asiatic theater of war and in the European theater. So far, no Axis Power possesses territory or bases in the Western Hemisphere (Martinique and Guadeloupe possibly excepted). This means that so long as we hold bases in the enemy's sphere, and so long as we can deny him bases in the Western Hemisphere, we can carry the war to him but he cannot carry the war to us. Submarine operations off our coasts and occasional air raids on our coastal cities can be conducted from transoceanic bases, but at long range our enemies cannot undertake serious, prolonged, intensive and continuous offensive measures against us at home. So long, moreover, as we hold our overseas bases and keep the enemy from securing bases in this Hemisphere, the factories of our "Arsenal of Democracy," unlike those of any other warring nation, can operate without much fear of prolonged interruption.

Germany and Japan understand this. Their primary strategy has been, therefore, to reduce the bases on which the power of the United Nations depends in the European theater and in the Far Eastern theater. The greatest, most heavily defended and most important of these bases – perhaps the only one which is absolutely indispensable to victory and which must be held at all costs if we are to avert defeat – is the British Isles. As soon as we entered the war, then, we at once took steps to make absolutely sure that Britain will not be cut off. We speeded up the strengthening of Iceland as an air and naval base. Even more significant, the first announced movement of American troops – the equivalent of a National Guard infantry division – was to Northern Ireland. In January this American force was moved rapidly and without loss to positions in Ulster near the naval and air bases which have been developed there by American contractors. They were sent not only to guard the bases; their presence in Northern Ireland was also expected to have some political effect upon Eire's attitude toward the war. Psychologically, too, the arrival of the vanguard of a new AEF was an important event in the continental "war of nerves." These men were the first, perhaps, of an increasing flow of troops to Britain and Ireland and Iceland. For if the war is to be won, most strategists agree, landings must some day be made, and Allied footholds and air bases established, on the coast of Western Europe.

In the Red Sea-Mediterranean area, meanwhile, American ships, technicians and men speeded work on a project which had been started before the first bombs dropped at Pearl Harbor – the development of a great supply, assembly and maintenance depôt in Eritrea. American technicians and supply experts were also flown in increasing numbers to Africa and the Middle East, where they undertook the development of transcontinental air routes, the construction of docks on the Persian Gulf, and the enlargement of the capacity of the Trans-Iranian Railway as a supply route to Russia and, via the Russian railroads, to China. This whole North African-Middle Eastern area constitutes another of the bases which we shall need in order to carry the war to the Axis. Now that we are at war we are developing it rapidly.

Though the bases of Allied power around the periphery of Europe still were holding at the moment these lines were written, and were being strengthened, the Japanese conquests in the Western Pacific had reduced the number of the bases which we had hoped to be able to use offensively against Japan.

The Japanese assault upon Pearl Harbor, a modern duplicate of the attack on Port Arthur in the Russo-Japanese War, was disastrous in its consequences, though not so disastrous as much loose talk might indicate. We already had transferred to the Atlantic, before that date, a considerable number of ships formerly in the Pacific. We had done this for several reasons – because of the completion of the German battleship Tirpitz and the aircraft carriers Graf Zeppelin and Deutschland; because the Scharnhorst and Gneisenau and the two German pocket battleships are powerful convoy raiders; because of the incipient menace of the French Fleet; and because of the necessity of strengthening the supply routes to Britain. We thus had accepted a quantitative naval inferiority to Japan. Pearl Harbor did not, therefore, fundamentally and permanently alter the strategic picture in the Pacific; that picture already had been altered by deliberate policy. But the loss of the battleships Arizona and Oklahoma, and the severe damage done to other capital and lighter units, reduced the ratio of our overall superiority vis-à-vis the combined Axis navies and in the Pacific further increased the Japanese superiority.

Japan's strategical plan, of which the attack on Pearl Harbor was an integral part, was boldly conceived and skillfully executed. Its outstanding characteristic was the same as has distinguished all the German operations – complete coördination of effort. Wake and Guam were captured (the former with unexpectedly heavy losses to the Japanese as a result of the brilliant defense by our marines) and our direct line of communications to the Philippines thus was severed. In the Philippines, the two principal airfields on Luzon, where we had been trying to build up a striking force of heavy bombers, were bombed heavily in a surprise attack launched from the Japanese bases on Formosa; and by the second day many of our bombers had been destroyed on the ground. The Philippines also were invaded at a number of points. Simultaneously Hong Kong and Malaya were assaulted.

The pattern of the invasion of the Philippines differed in only two principal respects from what had been expected. The Japanese utilized somewhat more force than had been thought possible; and the American Asiatic Fleet proved to be a more or less negative factor in the defense of the islands. Once the Japanese had established land-based airfields at Aparri, Vigan and elsewhere on Luzon, their huge transport fleets, heavily protected by fighting ships and planes, were able to disgorge troops almost at will. By the new year, in less than a month of combat, General Douglas MacArthur's delaying actions, fought with insufficient troops and inadequate air support, had played their part. Manila was given up and the siege lines were drawn across the difficult terrain of the Bataan peninsula, where a courageous handful of troops – soldiers, sailors and marines; Philippine Scouts and Philippine Army; regulars, National Guardsmen and selectees, some of them with only six months' training – were still fighting and dying as these words were written. American-officered Philippine troops also still held Northern Mindanao. But in general the Philippines could be said to be cut off and hopelessly surrounded. These islands, which "Teddy" Roosevelt once characterized as America's strategic Achilles heel, and which more recently we had hoped to use as an offensive base against Japanese lines of communication, had definitely become a sideshow in a greater game and had been written off.

Hong Kong, it had been hoped, could hold out for months rather than days. Its quick fall was followed by an amazingly rapid Japanese advance down the Malay peninsula. The subsequent fall of Singapore, with the capture of something over 70,000 British troops and much equipment, was the greatest single British defeat of the war. These were shocking blows to the strategy of the United Nations in the southwestern Pacific. They were accompanied by a Japanese penetration of Burma, followed soon by a break-through against the British line on the Salween River. At the same time another Japanese claw was reaching out toward the Netherlands East Indies. Following the same pattern of conquest which had given victory to the Germans – establishment of air superiority – Japan seized airfields at a series of strategic points and soon brought under her control nearly all the approaches to Singapore and all the entries into the South China Sea. Her amphibian operations were conducted with great skill and were carefully coördinated to air power. The underestimated Japanese airmen, too, did not restrict the demonstration of their capacity solely to Pearl Harbor, but also sank the British Prince of Wales and Repulse.

Despite the dispersed nature of these operations, the Japanese probably have not used more than 400,000 to 700,000 troops in the entire southwestern Pacific. However, the small parties that landed from transports in widely-scattered parts of the Malay barrier and swept aside light resistance,[i] were heavily supported by a major part of the Japanese Fleet, organized in task forces, and by overwhelming air superiority. There were other elements also in their successes. There were thorough training and excellent coördination, particularly in amphibian operations; fanatical courage and determination; and a willingness to take great losses in order to achieve great gains. As a result of these combined factors, the Japanese in three months of war surged over the Malay barrier, reduced Singapore, greatest base in the Eastern Seas, and stormed against the gates of Australia and India. Their victories have prolonged the war by postponing indefinitely any hope of our launching offensive operations against Japan from the southwestern Pacific. For over the most important bases in this area now floats the banner of the Rising Sun.

Japan's quick conquests are not to be attributed solely to Japanese strength and skill. They are also attributable to Allied weakness and unreadiness. The Japanese profited by surprise. They also profited by our mistakes. Our Asiatic Fleet, and most of the naval forces of the United Nations in the Orient, apparently adopted a defensive policy – at least until after the relief of Admiral Thomas C. Hart, the American commander, under General Sir Archibald Wavell, of the combined naval forces in the area. Except for a few submarine successes, our Asiatic Fleet, apparently in accordance with a deliberate decision of policy, made little attempt to fight off the Japanese landings in the Philippines; and though it is fair to note that the evacuation of Cavite was carried out skillfully, it must be added that evacuations do not win wars. What we were fighting for in the Philippines, and in the Outer Possessions of the Netherlands East Indies, was time. To delay the Japanese and to hurt them would thus have been worth the sacrifice of many ships. Yet in the first two months of war not a single American naval vessel had been reported lost in action with the enemy, except those destroyed at Pearl Harbor.

Now wars cannot be won without losing ships and lives. A more daring and costly policy in the Orient might have given us a commodity which is most precious in modern war – time – time to overcome the shock of surprise and the handicap of distance, time to compensate for at least Japan's initial advantages in holding an "interior position," time to organize convoy routes half as long as the circumference of the globe and three to twelve times as long as the Japanese communications, time to build up stores of supplies in Australia, Java, Burma and India and to transport precious reinforcements of all kinds to the theater of action, time for our offensive tactics to produce their full effect of attrition on Japan's all-out effort.

No matter how skillfully our naval power had been handled, however, it probably could not have saved Singapore. The fall of that stronghold was not due simply to lack of adequate naval power, but to gross air inferiority and (as at Pearl Harbor) to an obvious complacency and lack of forethought on the part of the British defenders. They seemingly might have made better use of the forces at their disposal than they actually did make. The Japanese generalship and troop training were both superior to the British. The enemy seems to have developed a form of infiltration tactics by lightly armed men – almost guerrilla units – which is peculiarly adapted to fighting in the tropics and especially in jungle areas. The British, unlike MacArthur's better acclimatized and better trained troops, apparently made the mistake – initially at any rate – of trying to use conventional Occidental methods of fighting in jungle country against an Oriental enemy.

The full story of those three months of tragedy remains to be told. Even now, however, it can be said with confidence that though the Japanese have won great successes, have severely shaken the prestige of the white man in the Orient, and have greatly increased the difficulty of our task, they are by no means unbeatable. There are other Far Eastern bases for us to use as springboards for attack upon them.

The first and main task is to halt the Japanese surge of conquest, if not at Java then on the coast of Northern Australia and in Burma. Our gigantic long-range convoys across the Pacific, unprecedented in the history of war, have begun to build up stockpiles of materials in Australia; and the supply routes have been strengthened by the garrisons we have placed on the islands along the way. But now that the Japanese are in possession of Malaya and the Indies, their need for oil and other raw materials is largely met, whereas we must transport most of our oil supplies to Australia. Because of this, Australia's rôle will be, for the time being, that of a defensive barrier rather than an offensive base.

Meanwhile we must look to the area India-Burma-China, to our mid-ocean bastion of Hawaii, to the Alaska-Aleutian area, and to the Russian bases in eastern Asia – specifically, Petropavlovsk on the Kamchatka peninsula – as the future springboards for the offensive operations against Japan which we must undertake if we are to be victorious. The pattern of our eventual victory has already, in part, been set; the Fleet's raid upon the mandated Marshall Islands follows the traditional strategy long ago envisaged in case of a war with Japan. Such offensive operations must be, surely will be, extended in scope and power. For this is a war for survival, and only by smashing assaults can we hope to save our lives. [Full Article]

HANSON W. BALDWIN, military and naval correspondent of the New York Times; author of "The Caissons Roll," "United We Stand!" and other works

© Foreign Affairs

July 1942

Hitler's Transfers of Population in Eastern Europe [Excerpt]

Hedwig Wachenheim

Beginning of Lebensraum, *the Nazi German expulsion of Poles from central Poland, 1939*

FRESH from his conquest of Poland, Hitler on October 6, 1939, announced to the Reichstag that there would be "a new order of ethnographical conditions, that is to say, a resettlement of nationalities in such a manner that the process ultimately results in the obtaining of better dividing lines." A day later he signed a decree transferring to the Reich all Germans who are "threatened with de-Germanization," and he entrusted to Heinrich Himmler, chief of the Gestapo, the duty of carrying out the resettlement program as Commissioner for the Strengthening of Germandom. So well did Himmler work that by March 1941 all German settlers beyond the Reich's new northeastern border and beyond the Carpathian Mountains, which are considered to be the Reich's strategical southeastern frontier, had been transferred to Germany.

Was this transfer of Germans to the Reich really based on a plan for new ethnographical divisions? The program was a tacit part of the Italo-German Pact of May 22, 1939.

Hitler's Transfers of Population in Eastern Europe [Excerpt]

Mussolini was eager to clear the provinces of Venezia Tridentina (Bolzano and Trento) of their German-speaking people. He had been unable to Italianize them in the course of 16 years, and the region's industrial capacity and position near the frontier of his new but dreaded ally meant that it was one of vital strategic importance to Italy. The program also figured tacitly in the Russo-German Pact of August 23, 1939. Stalin was glad to free his future border zone of a population which might be disloyal in case of war with Germany. Hitler had always assumed the rôle of "protector" over the German-speaking citizens of the smaller countries in Eastern Europe. As long as he hoped to acquire the territories on which they lived without having to wage a war against the Western Powers, he proclaimed the inseparability of blood and soil. But by April 1939, when he began to realize that Britain might really fight for Poland, he was ready to sacrifice the German outposts in Italy and in future Russian territory in order to gain Italian coöperation and Russian neutrality. Hitler held back from the resettlement plan as long as the German minority in Poland was needed to undermine that country. Then, after Poland's defeat, he announced it, not as a change of policy enforced upon him by circumstances, but as a "new order" for the benefit of all Europe....

... While western Poland was serving as the goal of the German westward migration, central, southern and eastern Poland were selected as the area towards which Europe's outcasts were to be directed.

How far these regions have been depleted by the three great eastward migrations cannot be said, for these movements were hidden by the Russian censorship. More than a million Polish soldiers and civilians, including 300,000 to 500,000 Jews, must have fled eastward and southward from the German onslaught in 1939. The Russians deported 2,000,000 Polish citizens to Asiatic Russia and Siberia after their occupation of eastern Poland. How many Poles, White Russians, Ukrainians and Jews were among them? Nobody, probably, knows. The number of people who fled from the Russian-occupied areas and from western Russia when the Russian armies were retreating in 1941 is also unknown.

The largest group deported to the Gouvernement General by the Nazis was made up of 1,500,000 to 2,000,000 Poles from the German-annexed areas. Second in number were the Jews. There were 200,000 Jews left in Germany, Sudetenland and Austria by the time Germany declared war on the United States.[xii] The Bohemian-Moravian Protectorate then contained at least 84,000. At the time of the annexation, 545,000[xiii] were in the annexed parts of Poland, most of them in the province of Lodz. Besides, there are approximately 6,900,000 Jews under German domination in the east.[xiv] How many of these were killed by the war, by starvation or by organized Nazi terror, and how many were able to flee into Russia or Turkey, or even into Italy, cannot be stated exactly.

In Germany and her five southeastern dependencies, where local anti-Jewish policy has been fully coördinated with the German, Jews are now concentrated in huts outside the cities or sent to labor or concentration camps. Many are deported to the Lublin "Reservation," in the Gouvernement General, or to the neighborhood of Pinsk. More recently they also have been sent to the ghettos of Kaunas and Minsk. Those in the camps and near Lublin and Pinsk have to work on roads and canals or on rivercontrol and swamp-draining projects. The rest live in ghettos isolated from the outside world.

Reports indicate that most of the Jews from the annexed parts of Poland have been deported to the Lublin Reservation, with the exception of 160,000 to 200,000 who are concentrated in the ghetto of Lodz. The number of Jews deported to the Gouvernement General or Ostland from old Germany, Austria, Sudetenland and the Protectorate is not under 40,000, by a very conservative estimate. In addition, Hungary deported at least 18,500 Jews to Galicia in 1941; 54,000 were dumped into the Ukraine from Rumania last fall; and this spring Slovakia seems to have begun sending her 70,000 Jews to Poland. But when no trains are available for deportation, or when Germany needs hands, this policy is shrewdly and coldly interrupted. Recently, Jewish artisans from the Ukraine have been sent into Germany proper.

It should be noted, however, that deportation to the Gouvernement General is not restricted to Jews. At least 30,000 Slovenes from Croatia have been sent there, as have Rumanians from Northern Transylvania. Recalcitrant Frenchmen from the occupied zone are among the latest arrivals.

The deportations do not represent merely a policy of racial and political hatred. Cheap labor is needed, particularly for vast canal-building and swamp-draining projects. Workers in Germany and the countries allied with the Reich would probably rebel if they were put at this work. In the "Annex" (Nebenland), as the Germans call the Gouvernement General, public morale is of no importance.

In contrast to the policy followed in the Protectorate, the Volksdeutsche in the Gouvernement General have not been made German citizens. In the hierarchical order established by the conqueror they form the second class, under the Reich Germans who govern the country. Third in rank are the Poles. Ukrainians, Ruthenians and even White Russians can be elevated above the rank of a Pole if their respective bureaus in Berlin agree. Volksdeutsche who have been convicted of committing hostile acts against the Reich after the 1939 campaign are degraded to the lowest rank, that of the Jews. The natives of the Baltic countries are treated slightly better than the Poles, because their police are needed to help guard the rear of the German army. [Full Article]

HEDWIG WACHENHEIM, former member of the Prussian Diet and official in the German Ministry of the Interior

© Foreign Affairs

October 1942

The Spirit of Resistance [Excerpt]

Victor Vinde

German control post on the Demarcation Line.

THE masses of the French people simply did not understand what was happening to them when the German military machine rolled across the Loire and, with hardly a pause, down to Bordeaux and the Pyrenees. In those horrifying days of June 1940 there was almost no news either on the radio or in the press. Almost nobody tried to analyze the causes of the disaster. The pain of the moment was too acute, the catastrophe was too brutal, to permit generalizations or long views; immediate personal worries monopolized the thoughts of almost everyone. France fell, and lay in a kind of stupor.

When people did think, it was not old Marshal Pétain alone who imagined that a new world was about to be born, and that it might not be such a bad one after all. The Marshal told the French people – and each one of them in his heart wished to believe it – that the Germans were, after all, men like other men; that peace could not at any rate be harsher or more terrible than war; and that the sacrifices which the Germans would exact would be only temporary. Sooner or later there would be a resurgence of French life and what had been lost would be regained. So the peasant returned to the land, ready to work to earn that peace which the armistice had brought dimly into view.

Only slowly and gradually, when it became apparent that the Germans had no intention of treating France as a free and independent country, did French resistance begin to take shape. The peasants in the occupied territory were the first to realize the fact. They had seen the Germans arrive, smiling and with hands outstretched; they had read the posters on the walls of the town halls inviting "the abandoned population to trust the German soldier;" they had been prepared to believe them. But the day after the entry of the German troops, the mayor of each community was summoned before the Kreiskommandant, usually a haughty reserve officer, to hear a lecture in broken French. While the mayor stood, the Kommandant told him that the Germans and the Führer wished the French no ill, but that from now on they would have to change their way of living. Frenchmen were lazy and dirty; this had to stop. In future, the roads and villages were to be kept spick and span. France was to be put on a rational basis of production, under German supervision. It was fallow ground; the Germans were going to see to it that it became fertile and productive.

This first contact with the occupation authorities brought a feeling of disillusionment to all the peasants in the occupied territory, and this grew into antagonism as the Germans started to interfere with their daily life. German time was imposed – two hours ahead of the sun – and a system of requisition and control established. The French peasant, always resentful of any interference either from above or from outside, began to hate the invader profoundly. Appeals from Vichy urging him to collaborate fell on deaf ears. The Germans had humiliated him, had intruded on his personal domain. This he would not accept and could not forget.

One or two German companies of troops settled down in each of a thousand little French villages. The town hall became the Orts-Kommandantur, the best buildings were used as barracks, and everywhere the nicest rooms were requisitioned for the officers and non-coms. Before dawn each morning the village would be wakened by the strident call of the bugle and, peering from behind their window curtains, the inhabitants could see the small garrison lined up on the main square of the village and could hear the shouted commands of the little Nazi lieutenant and watch the jerky motions of the soldiers. The peasant clenched his fists in silence. Later, when it was dark, he repaired to the nearby woods to oil the automatic gun which he miraculously had found on the road one evening in June and which he now was keeping for a better day.

The hostility between the French peasants and the occupying forces took on a new character as soon as the troops were withdrawn from the little villages and concentrated at strategic points throughout the country. This happened early in 1941, when fresh troops were needed for the Russian campaign, then already in preparation. From that time on the resistance of the peasants almost everywhere in occupied France took on the form of sabotage of agricultural production. It has continued and increased. Each farmer plants and cultivates only enough for his own immediate needs because he knows with absolute certainty that any surplus would be used to feed, not his starving compatriots, but the German Army. The repeated appeals of the old Marshal and of his associates for increased agricultural production have been in vain. Now that the French peasant has seen the enemy at close range he will never assist him in any way to dominate France.

The people of the cities took much longer than the peasants to realize that the Germans were oppressors and not collaborators. When the workers returned to their factories and found that their old labor organizations had ceased to exist they blamed the fact on some of their union leaders and on the former Socialist and Communist politicians who had betrayed them – or so they thought, for they had no newspapers of their own to give them the facts. "Why resist?" many of them said. "The first thing is to live." Soon, however, they learned who it was that was responsible for the way things were. It was the Germans who had ordered that wages should remain at the prewar level notwithstanding the great increase in the cost of living. It was the Germans who seized the cattle arriving at slaughter-houses in the cities and the vegetables and potatoes which were shipped to the central market in Paris. But the Germans ruthlessly suppressed any and every attempt at organization in the plants, and soon most of these were under complete German control: the French worker had no choice but to submit.

Businessmen and the well-to-do bourgeoisie were the slowest to comprehend and to react. Many of them regarded the defeat as punishment for those who had toyed with democratic ideas and had strayed from the traditional ways of healthy conservative politics. Others felt that France no longer was able to stand on her own feet and that she could recover her prosperity and greatness only by fitting herself into a new Europe under German leadership. They had lost all real faith in their country. The insidious semi-Fascist propaganda which much of the French press – and especially poisonous weeklies like Gringoire and Candide – had been spreading long before the war, had led many to believe that National Socialism was a doctrine which defended private property and promoted social order, and hence one which they might be able to accept, even welcome. Numerous business people, then, hoped to find some modus vivendi with the Germans.

This illusion did not last long except in a limited number of cases. Immediately after the armistice, the Germans began putting into effect a plan by which all French industry was transferred into German hands. The general procedure hardly was varied. When a French industrialist or merchant needed to transport merchandise or to obtain raw materials he got in touch with the proper German authorities. Within a short time a representative of some German business group was sent to see him. This group agreed to collaborate with him in exchange for a participation in the business. Those who refused were simply dispossessed. Thus all the most important French firms – chemical, metallurgical, textile, automobile, as well as the railroads and the Paris subway – passed under the control of the Germans. The great German trusts, beginning with the I. G. Farben, simply helped themselves to what they wanted. But the looting did not stop there. Small plants or business firms which were not worth bothering about in the eyes of German big business nevertheless aroused the greed of medium-sized German industrialists, and a swarm of "buyers" representing the latter descended upon occupied France as well as the unoccupied zone. The occupation authorities strongly encouraged this raid, and few concerns escaped. Today, almost half of the capital invested in French industry is "legally" held by the Germans. In case of a German victory it would remain in their hands. No German peace, however lenient, could ever be expected to free French business from this hold.

In consequence, nearly all French industry is at present working for Germany, turning out all sorts of equipment as well as arms and munitions. Uniformed German comptrollers direct and. supervise the workers in every factory. The French industrialist is merely a partner in his own business, often not much more than an employee. The factory owners and other business people who in the autumn of 1940 expected to get on with the Germans have had to abandon their hopes. The immense majority of them collaborate with the Germans because they cannot do otherwise. Of course there are some who believe in a German victory and think Franco-German collaboration is the only possible foundation for profitable business. Some actually desire a German victory. But these really are few. Most resent collaboration and regard it as simply a makeshift arrangement to be endured somehow until events take a better turn.

Most of the middle class quite early joined the anti-collaborationist ranks. This was especially true of the school teachers – both of primary and secondary schools – and of large numbers of university professors. Efforts have been made by the Marshal's friends, of course, and particularly by M. Abel Bonnard, the present Minister of Education, to remove those who were pronouncedly hostile to the policy of collaboration. In spite of these efforts the majority of the school teachers and professors, especially those belonging to the lower middle class, have continued to resist. The same cannot be said of some of the upper university professors, especially in the Faculté de Droit at Paris.

Churchmen were on the whole slow to reach a decision. The Catholic Church did not need to oppose Vichy; indeed, the French Government, far from trying to diminish the power or influence of the Church, solicited its support.[i] On their side, German authorities were wise enough not to interfere directly with the Church in France. But the neutral attitude which as a result the Church has adopted towards personalities and events since the armistice must not be mistaken for active approval of Vichy's policies, or even for friendly complicity in them. It must be said, however, that in the main the high clergy have remained personally loyal to the Marshal, even though some of them in private condemn M. Pierre Laval and his henchmen. The small clergy, on the other hand, and especially the country priests who live in close contact with their rural parishioners, appear to be decidedly hostile towards collaboration, even though at times they accept some of Pétain's political tenets.

The attitude of the Protestant Churches in France is harder to appraise correctly. As recently as a year ago, ardent supporters of Marshal Pétain could be found among members of the Reformed Church. Laval's rise to power, however, seems to have produced a change in those quarters. As for the French Lutherans, they could hardly remain indifferent to the Nazi attacks on their church in Norway and its fierce struggle for existence; this in turn developed and reinforced their own spirit of resistance.

At the beginning, French resistance sought rather timidly for means to express itself and undertake active work. The example of General de Gaulle and the information supplied in the French broadcasts from London certainly played an important rôle in crystallizing the determination of those at home not to accept Hitler's new order and not to be won over by Vichy to collaboration. I remember many evenings spent in little French farmhouses in occupied territory, listening with a group of peasants to the French voice coming over the air. Those who have not had that experience will never be able to grasp the enormous psychological influence of these voices. General de Gaulle soon became a kind of deity, to whom people listened almost religiously. The Germans naturally made intense efforts to jam the foreign broadcasts, but they were unsuccessful except in the large centers; and by means of them Frenchmen remained in constant contact with the outside world. Indeed, it is a usual experience to find that in the countryside the peasants know of some event in a distant part of the world 24 hours before the Berlin or Vichy press publishes the news of it.

Vichy has done everything it can think of to discredit the exiled General. Sometimes de Gaulle is pictured as a Free Mason and an enemy of labor; at others he is described as a mouthpiece for the royalists; at others he is called a Communist; and at others he is said to have joined with Jews and demagogues to plan the destruction of the French social hierarchy. The Germans naturally have given strong support in this campaign. They covered walls with posters in which General de Gaulle was accused of starving the French people because he did not protest against the British blockade. All sorts of absurd calumnies were directed against him in the German-controlled newspapers and in pamphlets. Yet no amount of slander could alter the fact that it was de Gaulle who had organized the continuation of French military resistance to the Nazis and who was fighting alongside of Great Britain and the United States. As such he was, and increasingly is, the symbol of eventual liberation.

It is interesting to note, by the way, that people show little interest in politics as such in either the occupied or the unoccupied zone. The one thing upon which they all agree is that they do not want to see the return of the men who ran French politics before the war. Men of all the parties – Socialists and Royalists, Communists and Conservatives – follow the Marshal and sing the praises of the invaders, just as men from all the parties fill the concentration camps and face the firing squads. Frenchmen who risk their lives every day to help liberate their country care little whether this man or that is a Communist or a Free Mason, a Jew or a Breton, a bourgeois or a laborer, a priest or an officer. They may worry about it later, when they have regained their freedom. But when German propaganda spreads rumors from London or New York of misunderstandings within the Fighting French movement, or tries to work up party feelings, the average Frenchman only smiles sadly.

Politics have been put aside; they simply do not exist. The one important thing is that the United Nations shall win the war and save the world. Whether a man is for that or against it is the sole criterion by which he is judged.... [Full Article]

VICTOR VINDE, for many years Paris correspondent of Swedish newspapers, including service after the fall of France in both the occupied and unoccupied zones; an editor of the Göteborgs Handels-och Sjöfartstidning

© Foreign Affairs

January 1943

America at War: The First Year [Excerpt]

Hanson W. Baldwin

REUTERS

THIS has been a year of hope deferred, of tragedy, of the most acute danger this nation has ever faced, a year of great defeats and great victories, a year in which the United States has found its soul, mustered its strength, organized its armies, and commenced its long, hard forward march to victory. It has been a year of crisis, but of crisis met, endured and passed. It has seen, probably, the turning point of the war.

This can be said because during the past summer and fall the enemy was held in check within the bounds of Europe and within the limits of the Western Pacific. As Churchill wisely warned, the American offensive in the Solomons and the Anglo-American campaigns in North Africa are not the beginning of the end; but they may mark, as he said, "the end of the beginning." Slowly but surely the strategic initiative is shifting to the United Nations. The future will depend more upon what we do than upon what the enemy does. We can still lose the war, but if we do so it will be because of our own mistakes and weaknesses, not primarily because of the enemy's strength. For the strength of the Axis is commencing to be outmatched and the inestimable advantages of the initiative are passing to our side.

The year began in disaster. The Japanese "sneak" attack on Pearl Harbor did much more damage than was admitted at the time. The Navy's report published a year later showed that eight battleships, ten other men-of-war, a floating drydock, and some 250 Army and Navy planes, were destroyed or damaged by the Japanese carrier-based air attack. Five of the battleships, the Arizona, Oklahoma, California, Nevada and West Virginia, were sunk or beached; three other battleships, the Pennsylvania, Maryland and Tennessee, and three cruisers, the Helena, Honolulu and Raleigh, were damaged. The Arizona blew up and was a total loss; the Oklahoma and the old target ship Utah-capsized and still lie keels-up in their berths near Ford Island; the destroyers Cassin and Downes blew up. But all the other ships, even including the minelayer Oglala which capsized, have been raised and have been or will be repaired. Plane losses and the small damages to installations have been made good long ago, and today "Pearl Harbor" is but an awful memory.

For six months after December 7, 1941, we went from bad to worse. But now at the year's end we have progressed to a position where we can undertake strategic offensives in both hemispheres. The size of the American Army and Navy has been more than doubled. Our global lines of communication have been maintained and strengthened and guarded by garrisons at strategic points. Close to a million Americans have been transported overseas. In this same year a number of important strategic areas have been lost by the Allies – Singapore, Burma, the Dutch East Indies, the "Donbas," part of the Caucasus. But others, the vital ones, have been held – the Middle East, India, China, Moscow, the bulk of the Caucasus oil areas, Britain, Alaska-Aleutians, Hawaii. Today, the United Nations are far stronger in numbers of men, ships and planes, in resolution, military leadership, organization and purpose, than they were a year ago. The enemy has been checked, even though not completely halted. With our allies we have commenced the long and sanguinary process of reconquering what was lost.

With this change in the strategic picture has gone a profound change in the art of war. Tactically, the defense has overcome many of the advantages enjoyed initially by the offense. What started in 1939 as a limited war became in 1942 a global one. Space, time and distance factors have intervened in the affairs of nations, and those which at first were amateurs in the art of war – the United Nations – are becoming professionals. Attrition practised by our side has replaced Blitzkrieg on the Axis side.

America at War: The First Year [Excerpt]

On land and at sea the defense is catching up with the offense. The quick victories of the past will no longer be possible for the Axis. The converse is also true, however. We must remember now when we are assuming the offensive that we cannot expect rapid triumphs over a defensive that has gained new strength. [Full Article]

HANSON W. BALDWIN, military and naval correspondent of the New York Times, recently returned from a tour of the Pacific; author of "The Caissons Roll," "Strategy for Victory" and other works

© Foreign Affairs

October 1943

Datum Point

Hamilton Fish Armstrong

REUTERS

OUR aim in this war is the complete material and psychological defeat of our enemies. We have rejected the idea of an armistice or negotiated peace and have pledged ourselves not to accept either at any stage or in any guise. When we have beaten Germany, Japan, Italy and their satellites, together or seriatim, into unconditional surrender, and while we are making sure that our accomplishment cannot be evaded or undone, we shall not recognize any limitations on our action except those imposed by our own consciences or any commitments except those which have been arrived at openly among the United Nations.

The outlines of the postwar world which we and our allies have already sketched constitute a pledge to and among ourselves alone. We may bungle the attempt to turn it into living reality. If so, we shall again suffer the lamentable consequences of our failure. But this time we are making our enemies no promises and shall not count on them to fulfill any part of a bargain. We on our side rely on ourselves alone – our own physical strength, our own strength of will. If we fail to keep the promises which we have made to ourselves and between ourselves we shall complete the destruction of our civilization by our own sole negligence and frivolity.

We hope to be able eventually to accept the peoples now our enemies as partners, and we are prepared to go as fast and as far as we safely can in making such a relationship with us seem reasonable and even attractive. But we fear that "eventually" is a long way off. In the interim, the one standard by which we shall measure every step will be whether it increases or diminishes our security. We shall try this time to remember how close we came to destruction and the grim sacrifices by which at the last moment we saved ourselves from it. Without vindictiveness but without apology or compunction we shall assign each of our beaten enemies his necessary rôle; and, provided we can match our perseverance to our present determination, we shall see that he carries that rôle through precisely, until such time as we may deliberately decide to modify it.

What does this mean, country by country?

It means that we intend to teach the German people beyond any chance of misunderstanding or later denial that they are not a race of supermen designated by some primordial decree to rule the world but instead a quite ordinary conglomeration of several racial stocks, without preternatural origins, with a number of unlovely traits as well as talents of a high order, and with a completely wrong belief that you can pound your neighbors into loving you as an apache pounds his woman into dazed rapture. We intend to see that the methods by which Germany regenerates herself confirm the lessons of her defeat. We hope that as a result of the dual demonstration Germans will understand that they are not unlike other nations and realize that in future they must cultivate something which they have always discounted in their attempts to wring satisfaction from an obscure destiny – the spontaneous esteem and collaboration of the rest of the world.

We are not so careless or unfair as to indict the whole German people for the specific crimes of some Germans. We do, however, indict them as a whole for having allowed arrogant thought and regardless action to secure a dominant place in their organized national life. We have only an academic interest in discussing whether the abdication of individual judgment which is responsible derives from a German inferiority complex or a German superiority complex, supposing the two are really different. We know that whichever it is, it has dogged the German people from the Valhalla of perpetual fights and feasts to the military councils of Potsdam, the beer halls of Munich, the frozen Volga and the grey village square where the French priest and postman are shot as a routine reprisal for some act of sabotage committed by persons unknown either to them or to the German officer who gives the command.

Some day, we must hope, the German nation will break loose from the ancient spell and cease to quiver between elation and despair, with acts of violence always the compensating outlet from either intolerable strain. Some day, we must hope, Wotan will yield to Apollo. Until we are sure that day has come we mean to curb at the source every manifestation of the traditional German spirit which can possibly bring ruin again to the quiet homes of peaceful peoples, near or far.

We do not underrate German culture, whether it comes to flower in German science or the glories of Goethe and Beethoven. Similarly, we think Germans should not underrate other cultures, and certainly not to the point where they feel entitled to tear them up by the roots and sow salt in the fields where they flourished. We cannot require Germans to think highly of Comenius or Chopin, Hus or Dvorak, Racine or Pasteur, Tolstoy or Tchaikovsky, Van Dyck or Erasmus; but we can require that they leave peoples which have produced men of genius like these to continue the peaceful enjoyment of their works and to continue adding diversifications and special beauties to our common civilization. We intend to do this. We recognize that we cannot re-orient the German mentality from without by force or effect a lasting change in the political and social organization of German society against the will of the effective majority of Germans. But we can create conditions in the world which are likely to make the majority of Germans decide in favor of letting other nations continue to live well as a condition precedent to themselves living better. We have various plans whereby in the course of time and with sufficient good will we hope that all nations may be enabled to live better. So far as the Germans are concerned, we think we are likely to make permanent progress only if we address them at the start wholly in their own familiar categorical imperative:

"Conquered lands – leave them! Armies – disband them! Stolen goods – return them! Prisoners – free them! Discriminations – repeal them! War factories – dismantle them! Nazi heroes – hang them! Food? After we have fed those you have starved! Forgiveness? When you have repudiated the conception of German destiny which leads you to act detestably. Respect and confidence? When new German professors teach new lessons from new textbooks to new generations of German children, new German philosophers expound a new anti-mystic in new treatises, new editorial writers use a new language of tolerance in new German newspapers, new German statesmen seek a new German destiny in a new conception of coöperation and mutual accommodation, new German legislators embody that new conception in a new policy, new German judges ratify it, new German diplomats practise it and the German people in their hearts approve it!"

We intend to teach the Japanese, who have not been defeated in modern history, that they can be defeated. We intend to drive out of their heads the same fixed notion of superiority which makes the Germans feel thwarted and restless in any world not yet conquered. We intend to demonstrate to them that their Emperor is not a god but a man of most fallible judgment; that his policies are not evolved in the remote stillnesses of Heaven but in the councils of palace sycophants and ambitious generals; and that they are founded on error and bring disaster.

As with the Germans, we think the most hopeful way of giving the Japanese their new and necessary sense of proportion is by practical demonstration. No matter how long it takes, we shall reconquer from Japan bit by bit all the territories which she has seized in this and previous wars and return them to their inhabitants, either at once or so soon as they can develop, with our help, the necessary capacities for self-rule. We shall disarm Japan immediately and completely. Her neighbors will admit her to a share in the co-prosperity sphere of the Far East when they feel she no longer interprets that phrase as meaning prosperity for herself and slavery for others. She will be allowed to share in the discussions and decisions of civilized international society when the nations which have preserved that society from Axis depredations are convinced that she has definitely abandoned force as a national policy and will seek a proportioned destiny through negotiation and collaboration.

The lesson which the Italians must take to heart is simpler because they are intrinsically weaker. It is that a second-class Power cannot be built into a master race by rhetoric, grimaces, blackmail and castor oil, and that attempts to ride to conquest on the coat-tails of others will end in humiliation and disaster no matter which of the major contestants wins.

When we call Italians to account for their merciless conduct in Ethiopia, Spain, Greece and Jugoslavia we shall not forget that Leonardo and Dante enriched the whole human race or that a generous idealism burned, not for Italians alone, in the hearts of Mazzini and Garibaldi. Nor, on the other hand, shall we forget that the Italian sovereign acquiesced in the coup d'état of 1922 and in Mussolini's countless subsequent illegalities and that the Italian people, with a painfully small number of honorable exceptions, stood negligently by for 20 years while the Fascisti destroyed one after another of the liberties which Mazzini and Garibaldi had won them. We shall not forget how many Italians of ancient name and large fortune wore the Fascist badge lightly in their buttonholes while Black Shirt gunmen were murdering in the streets and Mussolini was defiling the monuments of antiquity with puerile scribblings. We have seen pictures of the Italian Army goose-stepping in imitation of the enemies their fathers expelled from Lombardy and Venetia. We still remember, now that Mussolini's conquests have been wiped from the map, how pleased most Italians were with them while they were being won easily and cheaply.

The record seems to require that we do more than welcome the Italian people's eleventh-hour repentance. Their pride in having established the first totalitarian state in modern Europe and their support or tolerance of its violence at home and aggression abroad through two decades constitute something more than a juvenile escapade. When the Nazis have been pushed beyond the Alps we must examine with great care to see whether the new spokesmen who come to us in Italy's name have clean hands and whether their past records confirm their professions of devotion to constitutional methods of government. We have no interest in rehabilitating individuals who gambled wrong and now would like to recoup their losses out of the supposedly abundant funds of American generosity and naïveté. Only Mussolini and the chiefs of his jackal pack will require bodily punishment. But many more must be excluded forever from all share in the direction of Italian affairs and any Italian government must remain for a time on probation.

We shall not forget the lesser culprits. Hungarians, Bulgars, Rumanians and others have sold their services and reputations to the Nazis and Fascists, in some cases in return for parcels of territory stolen from neighbors with whom they had just signed treaties of faithful friendship and mutual aid. To these also we intend to make a memorable demonstration on behalf of international law, order and good faith. They will, of course, disgorge their stolen goods completely. But it will not be sufficient for them to do that, to dismiss their puppet dictators, to hang the officials who have joined the invaders in committing so many atrocities, and to profess repentance. They must give evidence, through acts, that in future it will be much harder than it has been in the past for some great neighbor to bribe them, or for new leaders of their own to manœuvre them, into wasting the savings of their simple and hardworking populations in foreign wars. We hope through general security measures to forestall small as well as large breaches of the peace. Even so, we think that before the nations of Eastern Europe can collaborate peacefully several of them will have to modernize the present feudal structure of their society and that living conditions in that neighborhood will have to be improved and equalized both as between classes and between nations. Perhaps this can be achieved more easily if the nations in question come together in one or more confederations. We shall not impede any such development and we shall be ready to give what material aid we can in the execution of these nec essary changes and improvements.

Presumably this statement of general intentions will be acceptable to most Americans. The differences of opinion crop out when one tries to particularize from the general, and especially when one begins to detail the lessons America must learn as well as those she must teach. Some people even feel quite sincerely that to think about those lessons or to outline the kind of world we are fighting for diverts energy from the fight itself and so constitutes a sort of sabotage.

There is, of course, a time for everything and first things come first. The American engineer dispatching a string of trucks northward from Zahidan, the marine landing at dawn on a beach on Guadalcanal, the pilot settling into the seat of his bomber for an attack on Düsseldorf, cannot be asked in that moment to think beyond the delivery into Russian hands of the tanks loaded on those trucks, the mopping up of the Japanese in the jungle behind that glimmering stretch of beach, the dropping of those bombs on the German factories. Nor can their colleagues back along the lines of communication to Washington, and the officers there where operational directives are issued, spend time, while the day's work is still to be done, thinking about things outside their own spheres of responsibility. But there is nothing incompatible between doing the day's work and having a clear idea as to why it is necessary. In fact, people who are not professional soldiers are apt to do the day's work better if they understand clearly the reasons which make it necessary and the results which will be its justification. The definitions must be made for them, however, by their political leaders. This falls in their sphere of responsibility. They must see that the war is conducted not simply so that it is won in the quickest time and with the least loss of lives but also so that it secures the fullest possible achievement of our broadest national objectives.

The objectives of a nation are not marked by a dot in time; they are continuous and developing. Nobody can suppose that consideration of any temporary factors of numbers, technics or logistics kept England erect when Nazi bombs rocked Westminster and Buckingham Palace and turned Coventry and Bristol to rubble; or decided de Gaulle to quit his country, family and army and continue France's war against Germany; or sent Mihailovitch and his Serb guerrillas into the mountains to fight planes and cannon with knives and rifles; or made the Czech nation ignore threats and punishments and continue to strike as individuals against the soldiers and police of their conquerors; or collected a Polish army from Russian prisons to take up the war again in the Middle East; or informed the Russians that at Stalingrad they would be impregnable. In each of these peoples there was a conviction that in the substrata of its national being runs a vital current which is not finite and perishable but continuous and self-renewing and that it will supply future generations with the substance of a better life long after the fragments of enemy shells have rusted away in the ground. Each of them has imagination; but none could imagine a time when it would cease to exist or, existing, cease to grow.

The United States has inherited wellsprings of that same national confidence from the days of Plymouth Rock and Lewis and Clark and Ellis Island. The country then was not abashed by the unknown, could look at its lengthening shadow and say boldly: "I change because I grow." Today those springs are riled. Contradictions and uncertainties attend the convulsive efforts of a giant nation which has been sprawling at ease on the floor to send the right message to its unaccustomed muscles, to draw itself erect, to substitute disciplined action for uncontrolled reflexes, and to strike coördinated blows at the enemies who had assembled unnoticed to destroy it.

The springs must and can be cleared. They must be cleared, both because we need confidence that we can create a secure and at the same time growing society if we are to set about planning it with sufficient intelligence and energy, and because unless that confidence exists we shall find the purely military victory harder to win. They can be cleared, by defining aims which are reasonable and possible and by taking, in company with our allies, the preliminary steps which will permit giving those aims eventual realization. Doubts are being sown by pessimists and traitors. Fundamental American principles are being misinterpreted by those too timid to hold them intact.

Monstrous world structures are being blueprinted by amateur engineers who seem to know everything except that nations are obstinately diverse. Milky illusions are being propagated by those who think of the war mainly as it seems to offer a lovely opportunity to transform the world into a neighborhood settlement house. And vague dreads and animosities are being inspired by those to whom it is only the opening phase of a new era of destructive social conflict and revolution. To such distortions the answer which will inspire confidence is not abuse, ridicule or violence but the presentation of a more detailed picture of our national destiny drawn on a larger canvas than any used yet.

The false prophets can be blanketed and the struggle in which we are engaged given more hopeful meaning if we will act imaginatively, yet soberly and with a sense of history, on the truth which Wendell Willkie uttered at Chungking: "The war is not simply a technical problem for tank forces; it is a war for men's minds." Since men's minds are not fettered by any limits of space or time our military strategy cannot accept such limits. When we repeat the current phrase that war is total, we mean – or ought to mean – that it is not merely total in its extent over the entire surface of the globe but total also in the inter-relation of what men remember from the past, what they do in the present and what they hope for the future.

It is a platitude of political discussion to say that a country should bring its responsibilities into balance with its physical powers. History furnishes plenty of horrifying examples of what happens, or might easily have happened, when it does not. But has the cardinal error of the United States been that it did not attempt to bring the two into balance? Does not history teach that the cardinal error of the United States was that it did not know where the line of its interests could be drawn?

The United States would be safe and respected, though hardly loved, if the whole area of its interests coincided with the zone of its power and if it remained constantly ready to use that power. But wishing will not make it so, and our adoption of a cautious policy of withdrawing our commitments to the outer limits of the range of our direct power will not protect those of our interests which lie beyond. It is beyond those limits, then, that foresight and the exercise of skill in the conduct of our foreign relations are most required. For it is in this outer zone that disputes which often do not seem to touch our interests originate and may grow into wars in which we may later be forced involuntarily to intervene. That outer zone, the writer believes, has no limits in the whole world.

If this thesis is true, we need urgently to arrange for our influence to be felt everywhere in the world, continuously and hence in time, despite the fact that in many parts of it we are unable to exercise power directly. And for this purpose we must accept partnership in a system of give and take, called by President Beneš "live and help live," not on a limited basis calculated by the limited range of our own individual power but on a universal basis calculated by the unlimited range of our national interest.

With whom shall we deal? With the nations that happen to live in our neighborhood, and as the leader of this bloc with other regional blocs? Or with one or two or three other Great Powers which in turn can exercise control over large areas of the world, so that together we can in fact control it all? Or with all like-minded Powers, the more the better? The writer believes that in the long run the United States will be stronger and safer in the larger group than in a bloc or a limited alliance. He believes that the general acceptance of a general relationship, with general though graduated responsibilities, offers the only basis for organizing world peace under the conditions produced by the development of science, communication and education, and that nothing but world peace is good enough for a World Power like the United States.

The cautious will say that half a loaf is better than no bread. But if the half loaf is not enough to support life, it is not worth risking much to gain. The American people will not find sufficient reward for their present sacrifices in being enabled to escape responsibility for helping prevent several small wars and then either perish or lose their way of life in another great war.

Neville Chamberlain said that the British people were not concerned with what was happening in a faraway land. As a result of that misapprehension Britain came as near to perishing as a nation can come and still manage to survive; and if Britain had perished we also should have perished, in one sense or another of the word. There is no faraway land. Our struggle to fix that fact in the public consciousness must not cease or falter. We must not proffer the American people half loaves or plan to accept half loaves on their behalf. On a half loaf they can subsist temporarily; they cannot live securely, nor develop as a nation the collective characteristics which in an individual we recognize give proportion, harmony and lasting satisfaction.

These pages are written in the conviction that our national future is bound up with the future of the whole world and not any single part of it; that it is possible at one time to learn from the past, work in the present and look to the future; and that it is necessary for our salvation that we do these three things together, do them on the scale indicated, and do them now.

Without a military victory there is no chance of a worthy peace. Without a worthy peace victory will have been worth winning in only a very limited sense. Whether or not the peace is worthy will depend on the coördinated action and common will of the United Nations – all of them – now and later. Unless we can reach clear understandings among ourselves now we are most unlikely to get them later. For the pattern of any future organization of the world will derive from the habits and instruments we create to deal with our present common peril, and if we cannot agree when the peril is instant and concrete how shall we agree when it has resumed the appearance of an abstraction?

These ideas are throbbing in the minds of millions of Americans, military and civilian alike, even as they concentrate on the day-by-day problems of the war. They crave to be told what it is they will get out of victory besides temporary survival. To let them see what they will get if they will assume the risks of peace as firmly as they have assumed the risks of war is not to divert their energies from the fearful tasks in hand – to give them, as one commentator naïvely put it, an opiate. On the contrary, it is to throw idle dynamos into action.

"From a high hill near the airdrome," wrote Byron Darnton from New Guinea in a last dispatch to the New York Times before his death there on October 18, 1942, "a man can see his countrymen building with blood, sweat and toil the firm resolution that their sons shall not die under bombs but shall have peace, because they will know how to preserve peace." Let the resolution of men at desks match the resolution of men under bombs. And let it be a resolution informed by the failures of the past and measuring without either foolish optimism or needless despair the difficulties and hazards of the future.

HAMILTON FISH ARMSTRONG, editor of FOREIGN AFFAIRS

© Foreign Affairs

January 1944

America at War: The End of the Second Year [Excerpt]

Hanson W. Baldwin

REUTERS

THE United States ended two years of war confident that the last phase of the struggle in Europe was starting. The protracted retreat of the German Army on the eastern front, the increasing tempo of Allied air raids on the Reich, the continuing failure of the German submarine war, the invasion and collapse of Italy, and particularly the Moscow conference justified that assumption. The Moscow Declaration that Britain, Russia and the United States would fight the war to unconditional surrender weakened Germany's hope of retrieving victory from defeat by political means. Specifically, the better understanding which the three Powers achieved there must have ended any idea she may have nourished that she could negotiate a separate peace with Russia. Since in addition it prepared the way for the international collaboration of the three Powers it must have dampened Germany's longer-range hopes also.

The last chapter nevertheless may be a long one. The end of the second year of war brings no evidence that Germany's military power has been broken. As Prime Minister Winston Churchill warned, the climactic year of 1944 is likely to be somber and bloody.

II

The great advance of the Red Armies on the eastern front was the most important event of the summer and fall of 1943, and as these lines were written it was continuing, though against stiffening opposition. Between July and late November the Russians reoccupied about 140,000 square miles of their own territory. The battle lines were approaching the pre-1939 Russian frontiers. Despite months of campaigning and great losses the Red Army evidently still possessed great offensive power.

Most of the credit for the Russian successes in the greatest campaigns in military history is Russian alone. Stalin has fashioned the Soviet states into a mighty machine for making war. The operations assigned this machine have often been prodigal in lives. But they have been effective because all the national energies of the Russian people were harnessed to a single end, and because no sacrifice was considered too great to achieve it.

The fact remains that the Russian victories of 1943 would not have been possible without aid from Britain and the United States. Lend-lease supplies, particularly in the category of automotive vehicles, gave the Russian Army much of its mobility, and American and British planes – many of them flown into Russia by various routes – helped materially in giving the Red pilots air superiority for the first time since the Russian campaign started. Shipments of lend-lease goods to Russia from the United States amounted to $3,287,047,000 by the end of September 1943, and of this total more than half had been shipped in the first nine months of 1943. The planes numbered 6,500. Among the other military items sent from the United States were 3,000 tanks, 125,000 sub-machine guns, 145,000 trucks, 25,000 jeeps, 200,000 field telephones and 700,000 miles of telephone wire. British shipments to Russia of vehicles, tanks, guns, ammunition, aircraft and industrial and naval supplies had reached the value of £179,000,000 by June 30, 1943. This figure is exclusive of the heavy expenses of delivery and convoy and also of the value of the large quantites of food, clothing and other civilian supplies sent to Russia on a credit system without any definite term for repayment. American and British food helped keep Russia from starving and American and British factories gave the Red Army some of its offensive punch.

But American and British aid to Russia was more important than even these figures indicate. Direct military intervention by the Allies on the battlefields of Europe diverted strong German forces from the Russian front, greatly weakened the German war potential and certainly was a vital factor in making it impossible for the Nazis to retain their hold on much of the richest Russian territory. The impossibility of measuring the effect of the Allied air raids on Germany and the Allied invasion of Italy in terms of miles gained by the Red Army has led certain elements in the United States to say that those operations were unimportant strategically. From the start, American Communists and fellow-travellers have been in the habit of belittling the American and British military effort. It seems time now to record that the Russian campaigns of the summer and fall of 1943 supplied direct evidence that the Allied operations in southern and western Europe had created a major diversion for Russia. The invasion and defeat of Italy forced Hitler to concentrate 20 to 25 divisions in that country. He also was compelled to reënforce the German divisions in the Balkans and to utilize for Balkan garrison duties the Hungarian and Rumanian units which otherwise would have been in action on the Russian front. How many German divisions the Allied operations actually drew away from the eastern front is not yet clear, probably not more than 5 or at the most 20. Our forces in Italy identified one or two crack German units which had been brought there from Russia. The important point to remember is that the majority of the enemy reënforcements sent to Italy and the Balkans probably were shifted from France or other occupied territories, and in turn were replaced from Germany's strategic reserve, thus restricting her ability to reënforce the Russian front. By December that strategic reserve was quite small.

The effect of the Allied air raids on western Europe was even more pronounced. These raids became so serious that Germany had to withdraw the bulk of her fighter planes from the eastern front. In consequence, our bombers in their raids over Europe in the latter half of 1943 faced two to three times as many German fighters as the Red Army encountered on the entire Russian front. In addition, units of the Luftwaffe were shifted from Russia to the Mediterranean. These shifts in German air power, in conjunction with the delivery of American and British planes to Russia as part of lend-lease aid, enabled the Russians during 1943 to secure air superiority except in localized sectors where the Nazis thought it important to make a great temporary effort. Thus it is fair to say that two of the important factors in the German retreat in Russia in 1943 – German air weakness in that theater and lack of German reserves – were the direct effect of Allied efforts. Nor can a third effect be ignored, though it was less direct and obvious. The bombardment of Germany without any question decreased her war potential, limited and in certain cases sharply curtailed her industrial output, damaged her communications, hampered her transportation and had devastating effects on the morale of her population. All this diminished the Reichswehr's strategic mobility and kept out of the hands of the German soldiers many weapons which they would otherwise have had at their disposal in fighting the Russian armies....

III

The climax of Allied operations in the Mediterranean came on September 3 with the collapse of Italy. The Badoglio Government, which assumed power when the "Sawdust Caesar" was deposed by a palace revolution on July 25, did not wait for the end of the 38-day Sicilian campaign to ask for the terms of surrender. After protracted negotiations, an armistice was signed on September 3, the very day British troops of the Eighth Army (General Sir Bernard L. Montgomery commanding) were ferried across the Strait of Messina to land on the Calabrian "toe" of Italy. The terms of the armistice, though not yet made public, evidently involved the cessation of all Italian fighting against the Allies, the surrender of as much of the Italian fleet as possible, Italy's adherence as a "co-belligerent" to the Allied cause, and the use of Italian troops against the Germans.

No major American units took part in the relatively small-scale invasion of Calabria across the Strait of Messina. But early in the morning of September 9, six days later, and 12 hours or so after the announcement of the Italian armistice (it was signed on September 3, but public announcement was delayed to secure the greatest military advantage), a combined Anglo-American army landed on the sandy shores of the Gulf of Salerno, some 30 to 35 miles below Naples. Lieutenant-General Mark Wayne Clark commanded this army, which, although it was known as the Fifth American Army, was composed almost equally of British and American divisions. Salerno was selected because it was the only practical landing beach within fighter range (extreme fighter range, at that) of Allied air bases in Sicily and extreme southern Italy. It had apparently been hoped that merely Italian coast defense troops would be encountered and that these would offer no great resistance. But Germans had replaced the Italians some days before, perhaps because of a "leak" in the Allied plans but more likely because obviously the Salerno beaches were the only possible place, south of Rome, where a landing was practicable. Apparently, also, the Allies miscalculated the strength of the German forces south of Rome and their ability to concentrate quickly.

What happened is now history. The Allied strategic plan involved some risk, since the landing was at the extreme range of fighter aircraft. Also, the Germans are an alert enemy and the terrain of most of Italy is mountainous. We were too sanguine in our hopes. The landing of the Eighth Army in Calabria – and subsequently at Taranto and Brindisi on the Italian "heel" – was intended to draw German units into southern Italy. The troops landed at Salerno, much further north, would be able, it was hoped, to slice across the peninsula and cut those German troops off.

But at Salerno the Germans had the great advantage of holding the wooded and precipitous heights around a saucer-shaped beach; their guns could fire downward into our concentrations and could command some of our landing places. There followed a battle which is rightly called "bloody Salerno." It was probably the hardest struggle in which American troops have yet been engaged in the European phase of this war, and one which we nearly lost. The vestigial glories of great empires of the past formed a picturesque setting for the bitter and costly action. "G.I.'s" bivouaced literally in marble halls and amid the ruined columns of Paestum, and their course toward Naples led them over the beautiful Sorrentine peninsula and past Pompeii and Herculaneum.

America at War: The End of the Second Year [Excerpt]

... General Clark has said that the situation at Salerno was never desperate. In retrospect it does seem likely that A.F.H.Q. in Algiers viewed it overanxiously. Nevertheless, the situation was serious, serious enough to warrant a comparison between Salerno and Gallipoli. In some sectors both Americans and British were pressed back to the beaches – almost to the water's edge. The casualties were heavy, and for a time the British and American forces were almost cut off from each other. The naval armada offshore, however, opened up with everything it had; carrier-based planes were active; and the Northwest African Air Force on September 14 flew 1,888 sorties over the battle area – more than one a minute – and dropped an average of nine-tenths of a ton of bombs on the German positions every minute. That day and the next saw the Nazi tide stemmed and led to the enemy retreat.

The battle was not won by any one arm alone. It was won only by the most careful coördination of each service with the other, and the most complete teamwork of each Navy and the troops of each nation with the Navy and troops of its ally. The cost was high, probably higher to the British than to the Americans, for the British – contrary to the impression of most Americans – had as many men at Salerno as the Americans did and held an even hotter sector. Ships were damaged and sunk, some of them by the Germans' new weapon, the controlled glide bomb (one of which is believed to have sunk the Italian battleship Roma as she was escaping to Malta). Losses in matériel were heavy.

We learned bitter lessons in the school of bloody experience.

One of them was the necessity of getting tanks ashore in the early stages of a landing. Another was the old, old lesson – so often repeated in this war – of the absolute necessity of competent leadership. An American Corps Commander and several general officers and colonels were relieved in action and some of them were demoted. We learned the need for quicker decision. A large force of heavy bombers was detached from the Eighth Air Force in Britain and sent all the way to the Mediterranean to assist at Salerno; but they arrived in the theater after the crisis of the battle was past. We learned again what had always been known but can easily be forgotten – the immense difficulty of making good a foothold on a shore strongly held by a determined foe.

Once the beachhead had been made good, General Clark's forces joined hands across southern Italy with the small Eighth Army forces which had pushed up the heel and toe of Italy against slight German opposition. The Nazis not only eluded the trap we had set for them, but almost baited it for us. They had suffered heavy casualties, however; they had failed to eliminate our beachhead; and, pivoting on the Sorrentine peninsula, they swung back their Adriatic Sea flank and commenced a slow and fighting retreat to and beyond Naples. Naples was captured on October 1 after considerable difficulties, but the water-front facilities had been thoroughly blasted by bombs and demolitions and the harbor was a tangle of wrecked shipping. The water supply of the city had also been destroyed and the inhabitants were starving. We began to experience both the liabilities and the assets of conquest....

... Progress in Italy at the time of writing is slow and may so continue. Weather, terrain and unexpectedly heavy enemy resistance are in part responsible. It is also true, however, that the strategic spotlight in Europe is shifting, that the Mediterranean is becoming a secondary theater. We therefore are trying to accomplish our remaining objectives in Italy (the immediate one is undoubtedly to capture Rome) with the utmost economy of force, so that our main effort elsewhere will not be reduced in strength.

The principal strategic objectives of the Allies in the Mediterranean were three: (1) the conquest of North Africa and the opening of the Mediterranean to Allied shipping; (2) the elimination of Italy from the war; (3) the seizure of Italian air bases for use in an air offensive against southern Germany. The capture of Foggia and Naples meant that all of these objectives had been achieved. What remained to be done in Italy was aftermath and to some extent anticlimax....

... As the year 1943 approaches its end the global strategic picture is more encouraging than at any time since the United States entered the war. Everywhere the United Nations have the initiative; everywhere the enemy is suffering defeat. Nowhere as yet, however, have the defeats been decisive. The enemy still is strong. If the war in Europe is to end in 1944, Britain and the United States probably will have to cap their entire strategical effort by a successful cross-Channel invasion. That is a venture which can, but must not, fail. It will usher in hard and bloody fighting. In the Pacific, the major strategic offensive which the Allies are now starting will assume weight and impetus during 1944. Its progress should determine in large measure the duration of the Pacific phase of the war. 1944 will indeed be a climactic year. [Full Article]

HANSON W. BALDWIN, military and naval correspondent of the New York Times; author of "The Caissons Roll," "Strategy for Victory" and other works

© Foreign Affairs

July/August 2013

The Road to D-Day [Excerpt]

Rick Atkinson

CAPTAIN J. L. EVANS / GETTY

Eurotrip: a British solider prepares for D-Day, May 1944

... on Monday morning, May 15, [1944] ... at St. Paul's School on Hammersmith Road, in western London ... , the greatest Anglo-American military conclave of World War II gathered on the war's 1,720th day to rehearse the deathblow intended to destroy Adolf Hitler's Third Reich. Admirals, generals, field marshals, logisticians, and staff wizards by the score climbed from their limousines and marched into a Gothic building of red brick and terra cotta, where American military police – known as "Snowdrops" for their white helmets, pistol belts, leggings, and gloves – scrutinized the 146 engraved invitations and security passes that had been distributed a month earlier. Then, six uniformed ushers escorted the guests, later described as "big men with the air of fame about them," into the Model Room, a cold and dimly lit auditorium with black columns and hard, narrow benches reputedly designed to keep young schoolboys awake.

Top-secret charts and maps now lined the Model Room. Since January, the school had served as the headquarters for the British 21st Army Group, and here the detailed planning for Operation Overlord, the Allied invasion of France, had gelled. As more senior officers found their seats in Rows B through J, some spread blankets across their laps or cinched their greatcoats against the chill. Row A, 14 armchairs arranged elbow to elbow, was reserved for the highest of the mighty, and now these men began to take their seats. The British prime minister, Winston Churchill, dressed in a black frock coat and puffing his usual Havana cigar, entered with the supreme allied commander, General Dwight Eisenhower. Neither cheers nor applause greeted them, but the assembly stood as one when George VI strolled down the aisle to sit on Eisenhower's right. Churchill bowed to his monarch, then resumed puffing his cigar....

AN UGLY PIECE OF WATER

Cometh the hour, cometh the man: at 10 AM, Eisenhower rose to greet the 145 comrades who would lead the assault on "Fortress Europe." Behind him in the cockpit of the Model Room lay an immense plaster relief map of the Normandy coast, where the river Seine spilled into the Atlantic. Thirty feet wide and set on a tilted platform visible from the back benches, this apparition depicted, in bright colors and on a scale of six inches to the mile, the rivers, villages, beaches, and uplands of what would become the world's most famous battlefield. A brigadier wearing skid-proof socks and armed with a pointer stood at port arms, ready to indicate locales soon to achieve household notoriety: Cherbourg, Saint-Lo, Caen, Omaha Beach.

With only a hint of his famous grin, Eisenhower spoke briefly, a man "at peace with his soul," in the estimate of a U.S. admiral in attendance. He hailed king and comrades alike "on the eve of a great battle," welcoming them to the final vetting of an invasion blueprint two years in the making. A week earlier, he had chosen June 5 as D-Day. "I consider it to be the duty of anyone who sees a flaw in the plan not to hesitate to say so," Eisenhower said, his voice booming. "I have no sympathy with anyone, whatever his station, who will not brook criticism. We are here to get the best possible results." The supreme commander would remain preoccupied for some weeks with the sea and air demands of Operation Overlord, as well as with sundry political distractions, so he had delegated the planning and conduct of this titanic land battle in Normandy to a British officer, General Bernard Montgomery.

A wiry, elfin figure in immaculate battle dress and padded shoes, Montgomery popped to his feet, pointer in hand. His narrow vulpine face was among the British Empire's most recognizable, a visage to be gawked at in Claridge's or huzzahed on the Strand. But before he could utter a syllable, a sharp rap sounded. The rap grew bolder; a Snowdrop flung open the Model Room door, and in swaggered Lieutenant General George Patton, a ruddy, truculent American Mars, newly outfitted by those Savile Row artisans in a bespoke overcoat, bespoke trousers, and bespoke boots. Never reluctant to stage an entrance, Patton had swept through London in a huge black Packard, bedizened with three-star insignia and sporting dual Greyhound bus horns. Ignoring Montgomery's scowl, Patton found his seat in the second row and sat down, eager to take part in a war he condemned, without conviction, as "goddamned son-of-bitchery." "It is quite pleasant to be famous," Patton had written his wife, Beatrice. "Probably bad for the soul."

With a curt swish of his pointer, Montgomery stepped to the great floor map. Glancing at his notes – 20 brief items, written in his tidy cursive on unlined stationery – Montgomery began in his reedy voice, each syllable as sharply creased as his trousers. "There are four armies under my command," he said, two composing the assault force into Normandy and two more to follow in exploiting the beachhead. "We must blast our way on shore and get a good lodgement before the enemy can bring sufficient reserves to turn us out," he continued. "Armored columns must penetrate deep inland, and quickly, on D-Day. This will upset the enemy plans and tend to hold him off while we build up strength. We must gain space rapidly, and peg out claims well inland."

The Bay of the Seine, which lay within range of almost 200 fighter airfields in the United Kingdom, had been designated as the invasion site more than a year earlier for its flat, sandy beaches and its proximity to Cherbourg, a critical French port needed to supply the invading hordes. True, the Pas-de-Calais coastline was closer, but it had been deemed "strategically unsound" because the small beaches there not only were exposed to storms in the English Channel but also had become the most heavily defended strands in France. Planners under the capable British lieutenant general Frederick Morgan had scrutinized other possible landing sites, from the French region of Brittany to the Netherlands, and found them wanting. Secret missions to inspect the Overlord beaches, launched from tiny submarines during the dark of the moon in what the Royal Navy called "impudent reconnaissance," had dispelled anxieties about quicksand bogs and other perils. As proof, commandos brought back Norman sand samples in buckets, test tubes, and Durex condoms.

The location of the landings was crucial, for if Overlord failed, the entire Allied enterprise faced abject collapse. But before the invading force could take any territory, it would have to contend with "an ugly piece of water called the Channel," as the official U.S. Army history of the invasion would later describe it. The English Channel was only 21 miles wide at its narrowest point. Yet for nearly a thousand years, invading armies facing a hostile shore across it had found more grief than glory. "The only solution," one British planner had quipped, "is to tow the beaches over already assaulted." The U.S. War Department had even pondered tunneling beneath the seabed: a detailed study deemed the project "feasible," requiring one year and 15,000 men to excavate 55,000 tons of spoil. Wiser heads questioned "the strategic and functional" complexities, such as the inconvenience of the entire German Seventh Army waiting for the first tunneler to emerge. The study was shelved.

Montgomery's presentation focused mostly on the technical details of the landings, but the general closed it on a different note. "We shall have to send the soldiers into this party seeing red," he declared, eyes aglint. "Nothing must stop them. If we send them into battle this way, then we shall succeed." After lunch and a number of briefings by other officers, Eisenhower stood for a few words of thanks, noting that Hitler had "missed his one and only chance of destroying with a single well-aimed bomb the entire high command of the Allied forces." Churchill gave a brief valedictory, grasping his coat lapels in both hands. "Let us not expect all to go according to plan. Flexibility of mind will be one of the decisive factors," he said. "Risks must be taken." He bade them all Godspeed. "I am hardening on this enterprise. I repeat, I am now hardening toward this enterprise."

Never would they be more unified, never more resolved. They came to their feet, shoulders squared, tramping from the hall to the limousines waiting on Hammersmith Road to carry them to command posts across the United Kingdom. Ahead lay the most prodigious undertaking in the history of warfare.

"RAMMING OUR FEET IN THE STIRRUPS"

Shortly after 6 PM, Eisenhower sped southwest through London in his chauffeured Cadillac, drawing deeply on a cigarette. In these fraught times, he often smoked 80 Camels a day, aggravating the throat and respiratory infections that had plagued him all spring. He also suffered from high blood pressure, headaches, and ringing in one ear; he had even begun placing hot compresses on his inflamed eyes. "Ike looks worn and tired," his naval aide, Commander Harry Butcher, noted in mid-May. "The strain is telling on him. He looks older now than at any time since I have been with him." The supreme commander was 53 years old.

As the dreary suburbs rolled past, Churchill's final remark at St. Paul's gnawed at Eisenhower: "I am now hardening toward this enterprise." The tentative commitment and implicit doubt seemed vexing, although Churchill had never concealed either his reluctance to risk calamity in a cross-channel attack or his dismay at the cautionary experience of Anzio, where four months after that invasion a large Anglo-American force remained bottled up and was shelled daily in a pinched beachhead. Yet for Overlord, the die was cast, spelled out in a 30-word order to Eisenhower from the Combined Chiefs of Staff, his superiors in Washington and London: "You will enter the continent of Europe and, in conjunction with the other united nations, undertake operations aimed at the heart of Germany and the destruction of her armed forces." Now was the time, as Eisenhower put it, for "ramming our feet in the stirrups."

For years, he had pondered just how to successfully enter the continent of Europe — first as a War Department planner; next as the senior American soldier in London in the spring and summer of 1942; then as the general superintending the invasions of North Africa, Sicily, and mainland Italy; and now as the commander of what was officially known as the Supreme Headquarters Allied Expeditionary Force. No one knew the risks better. No one was more keenly aware that three times the Germans had nearly driven Allied landings back into the sea – on Sicily, at Salerno, and at Anzio.

Growing in stature and confidence, Eisenhower had become the indispensable man, so renowned that a Hollywood agent had recently offered $150,000 for the rights to his life (plus $7,500 each to his wife, Mamie; his mother; and his in-laws). "He has a generous and lovable character," Montgomery would tell his diary before the invasion, "and I would trust him to the last gasp." Other comrades considered him clubbable, articulate, and profoundly fair. His senior naval subordinate, Admiral Sir Bertram Ramsay, asserted simply, "He is a very great man." U.S. President Franklin Roosevelt had chosen him to command Operation Overlord in part because he considered him to be "the best politician among the military men." In a memorandum, Roosevelt described Eisenhower as "a natural leader who can convince other men to follow him."

Yet he had not convinced everyone that he was a great captain, a commander with the ability to see the field both spatially and temporally, intuiting the enemy's intent and subordinating all resistance to an iron will. Montgomery, whose ambivalence toward Eisenhower's generalship would only intensify, offered private complaints as well as praise: "When it comes to war," he told a colleague, "Ike doesn't know the difference between Christmas and Easter." Field Marshal Sir Alan Brooke, chief of the Imperial General Staff, confided to his diary an assessment of the supreme commander's role at St. Paul's: "No real director of thought, plans, energy or direction! Just a coordinator – a good mixer, a champion of inter-allied cooperation, and in those respects few can hold a candle to him. But is that enough? Or can we not find all the qualities of a commander in one man?"

Eisenhower sensed such doubts, and perhaps harbored a few himself. In his own diary, he lamented the depiction of him in British newspapers as an administrator rather than a battlefield commander. "They dislike to believe that I had anything particularly to do with campaigns. They don't use the words 'initiative' and 'boldness' in talking of me," he wrote. "It wearies me to be thought of as timid, when I've had to do things that were so risky as to be almost crazy. Oh, hum."

He had indeed taken risks, crazy risks, but more lay dead ahead. Eisenhower was neither a philosopher nor a military theorist. But he believed that too few commanders grappled with what he called "subjects that touch the human soul – aspirations, ideals, inner beliefs, affection, hatreds." On such broken ground during the coming weeks and months, his captaincy and his cause would be assayed. For more than any other human enterprise, war revealed the mettle of men's souls.

Rick Atkinson

"BRITAIN IS NOW OCCUPIED TERRITORY"

By the tens of thousands, souls in olive drab poured into the United Kingdom. Since January, the number of GIs had doubled to 1.5 million, a far cry from the first paltry tranche of 4,000 in early 1942. Of the U.S. Army's 89 divisions, 20 now could be found in the United Kingdom, with 37 more either en route or earmarked for the European theater. Through Liverpool they arrived, and through Swansea, Cardiff, Belfast, Avonmouth, Newport. But most came into Glasgow and adjacent Greenock, more than 100,000 in April alone, 15,000 at a time on the two Queens – Elizabeth and Mary – each of which could haul an entire division and outrun German U-boats to make the crossing from New York in five days.

Down the gangplanks they tromped, names checked from a clipboard, each soldier wearing his helmet, his field jacket, and a large celluloid button color-coded by the section of the ship to which he had been confined during the passage. Soldiers carried four blankets apiece to save cargo space, while deluded officers could be seen lugging folding chairs, pillowcases, and tennis rackets. A brass band and Highland pipers greeted them on the dock; Scottish children raised their arms in a V for "Victory." Combat pilots who had fulfilled their mission quotas and were waiting to board ship for the return voyage bellowed, "Go back before it's too late!" or "What's your wife's telephone number?"

Just over eight million men had been inducted into the U.S. Army and Navy during the past two years – 11,000 every day. The average GI was 26 years old, born the year that "the war to end all wars" ended, but manpower demands in this global struggle meant the force was growing younger: henceforth, nearly half of all U.S. troops arriving to fight in Europe in 1944 would be teenagers. One in three GIs had only a grade school education, one in four held a high school diploma, and slightly more than one in ten had attended college for at least a semester. War Department Pamphlet 21-13 would assure them that they were "the world's best paid soldiers." A private earned $50 a month, a staff sergeant $96. Any valiant GI awarded the Medal of Honor would receive an extra $2 each month.

The typical U.S. soldier stood five feet eight inches tall and weighed 144 pounds, but physical standards had been lowered with respect to defects that once would have kept many young men out of uniform. A man with 20/400 vision could now be conscripted if his sight was correctable to at least 20/40 in one eye; toward that end, the armed forces would make 2.3 million pairs of eyeglasses for the troops. The old jest that the army no longer examined eyes but instead just counted them had come true. A man could be drafted if he had only one eye, or was completely deaf in one ear, or had lost both external ears, or was missing a thumb or three fingers on either hand – including a trigger finger. Earlier in the war, a draftee had had to possess at least 12 of his original 32 teeth, but now he could be utterly toothless. After all, the government had drafted a third of all the civilian dentists in the United States; collectively, they would extract 15 million teeth, fill 68 million more, and make 2.5 million sets of dentures, enabling each GI to meet the minimum requirement of "masticating the Army ration."

A revision of mental and personality standards was also under way. In April 1944, the U.S. War Department decreed that inductees need have only a "reasonable chance" of adjusting to military life, although psychiatric examiners were advised to watch for two dozen "personality deviations," including silly laughter, sulkiness, resentfulness of discipline, and other traits that would seemingly disqualify every teenager in the United States. In addition, the army began drafting "moderate" obsessive-compulsives, as well as stutterers. Men with malignant tumors, leprosy, or certifiable psychosis still were deemed "nonacceptable," but by early 1944, 12,000 venereal disease patients, most of them syphilitic, were inducted each month and rendered fit for service with a new miracle drug called penicillin.

Nearly 400,000 prefabricated huts and 279,000 tents had been erected to accommodate the Yank horde, supplementing 112,000 borrowed British buildings and 20 million square feet of storage space. GIs called this new world "Spamland," but the prevailing odor came from the burning feces in the army's coal-fired incinerators.

No alliance in the war proved more vital or enduring than that of the English-speaking peoples, but this vast American encampment strained the fraternal bond. "You may think of them as enemy Redcoats," each arriving GI was advised in a War Department brochure, "but there is no time today to fight old wars over again or bring up old grievances." Detailed glossaries translated English into English: chemist/druggist, geyser/hot-water heater, tyre/tire. Disparities in pay caused resentment; a GI private earned triple what his tommy counterpart drew, and the U.S. staff sergeant's $96 monthly salary was equivalent to a British captain's. The U.S. Army tried to blur the difference by paying GIs twice a month. But British penury was as obvious as the pubs that required patrons to bring their own beer glasses, or the soap shortage that caused GIs to call the unwashed United Kingdom "Goatland," or the fact that British quartermasters stocked only 18 shoe sizes, compared with the 105 provided by the U.S. Army.

American authorities urged tolerance and gratitude. "It is always impolite to criticize your hosts," a guide to the United Kingdom advised GIs. "It is militarily stupid to insult your allies." Not least important, British producers stocked the American larder and supply depot with 240 million pounds of potatoes, a thousand cake pans, 2.4 million tent pegs, 15 million condoms, 260,000 grave markers, 80 million packets of cookies, and 54 million gallons of beer.

The British displayed forbearance despite surveys revealing that less than half viewed the Americans favorably. "They irritate me beyond words," one housewife complained. "Loud, bombastic, bragging, self-righteous, morals of the barnyard, hypocrites" – these were among the terms Britons commonly used to described the GIs, according to one survey. Meet the Americans, a manual published in London, included chapters titled "Drink, Sex and Swearing" and "Are They Our Cousins?" An essay written for the British army by the anthropologist Margaret Mead sought to explain "why Americans seem childish." George Orwell groused in a newspaper column that "Britain is now Occupied Territory."

Occasional bad behavior reinforced the stereotype of boorish Yanks. GIs near Newcastle killed and ate the royal swans at the king's summer palace. Paratroopers from the 101st Airborne used grenades to fish in a private pond, and bored soldiers sometimes set haystacks ablaze with tracer bullets. Despite War Department assurances that "men who refrain from sexual acts are frequently stronger, owing to their conservation of energy," so many GIs impregnated British women that the U.S. government agreed to give local courts jurisdiction in "bastardy proceedings"; child support was fixed at a pound per week until the little Anglo-American turned 13, and 5 to 20 shillings weekly for teenagers. Road signs cautioned, "To all GIs: please drive carefully, that child may be yours."

Both on the battlefield and in the rear, the transatlantic relationship would remain, in one British general's description, "a delicate hothouse growth that must be carefully tended lest it wither away." Nothing less than Western civilization depended on it. As American soldiers by the boatload continued to swarm into their Spamland camps, a British major spoke for many of his countrymen: the Yanks were "the chaps that [matter].... We couldn't possibly win the war without them."

GEARS OF WAR

On Tuesday, May 23, a great migration of assault troops swept toward the English seaside and into a dozen marshaling areas – Americans on the southwest coast, British and Canadians in the south – where the final staging began. Marching rates called for each convoy to travel 25 miles in two hours, vehicles 60 yards apart, with a ten-minute halt before every even-numbered hour. Military police wearing armbands specially treated to detect poison gas waved traffic through intersections and thatched-roof villages. Soldiers snickered nervously at the new road signs reading "One Way." "We sat on a hilltop and saw a dozen roads in the valleys below jammed with thousands of vehicles, men, and equipment moving toward the south," wrote Sergeant Forrest Pogue, a U.S. Army historian.

Mothers held their children aloft from the curb to watch the armies pass. An old man "bent like a boomerang" and pushing a cart outside London yelled, "Good luck to yer all, me lads!" a British captain reported. On tanks and trucks, the captain added, men chalked the names of sweethearts left behind so that nearly every vehicle had a "patron girl-saint," or perhaps a patron girl-sinner. Almost overnight, the bright plumage of military uniforms in London dimmed as the capital thinned out. "Restaurants and night clubs were half empty, taxis became miraculously easier to find," one account noted. A pub previously used by U.S. officers for assignations was rechristened the Whore's Lament.

By late in the week, all marshaling camps were sealed, with sentries ordered to shoot absconders. "Do not loiter," signs on perimeter fences warned. "Civilians must not talk to army personnel." GIs wearing captured German uniforms and carrying enemy weapons wandered through the bivouacs so that troops grew familiar with the enemy's aspect. The invasion had begun to resemble "an overrehearsed play," complained the newspaper correspondent Alan Moorehead. Fantastic rumors swirled: that British commandos had taken Cherbourg, that Berlin intended to sue for peace, that a particular unit would be sacrificed in a diversionary attack, that the Wehrmacht possessed both a death beam capable of incinerating many acres instantly and a vast refrigerating apparatus to create icebergs in the English Channel. The U.S. military newspaper Stars and Stripes tried to calm jumpy soldiers with an article promising that "shock kept the wounded from feeling much pain." Another column in the paper advised, "Don't be surprised if a Frenchman steps up to you and kisses you. That doesn't mean he's queer. It just means he's emotional."

Security remained paramount. Planners had concluded that Overlord had scant chance of success if the enemy received even 48 hours' advance notice, and "any longer warning spells certain defeat." As part of Churchill's demand that security measures be "high, wide, and handsome," the British government imposed a ban in early April that kept the usual 600,000 monthly visitors from approaching coastal stretches along the North Sea, the Bristol Channel, and the English Channel. Two thousand counterintelligence agents sniffed about for leaks. Censors fluent in 22 languages, including Ukrainian and Slovak, and armed with X-Acto knives scrutinized soldiers' letters for indiscretions until, on May 25, all outgoing mail was impounded for ten days as an extra precaution.

Camouflaged inspectors roamed through southern England to ensure that the invasion assembly remained invisible to German surveillance planes. Thousands of tons of cinders and sludge oil darkened new road cuts. Garnished nets concealed tents and huts – the British alone used one million square yards – and even medical stretchers and surgical hampers were slathered with "tone-down paint," either Standard Camouflage Color 1A (dark brown) or SCC 15 (olive drab). Any vehicle stopped for more than ten minutes was to be draped with a net "propped away from the contours of the vehicle."

Deception complemented the camouflage. The greatest prevarication of the war, originally known as "Appendix Y," until given the code name Fortitude, tried "to induce the enemy to make faulty strategic dispositions of forces," as the Combined Chiefs of Staff requested. Fifteen hundred Allied deceivers used phony radio traffic to suggest that a fictional army with eight divisions in Scotland would attack Norway in league with the Soviets, followed by a larger invasion of France in mid-July through the Pas-de-Calais, 150 miles northeast of the actual Overlord beaches. More than 200 eight-ton "Bigbobs" – decoy landing craft fashioned from canvas and oil drums – had been conspicuously deployed beginning on May 20 around the Thames estuary. Dummy transmitters broadcast the radio hubbub of a spectral, 150,000-man First U.S. Army Group, notionally poised to pounce on the wrong coast in the wrong month.

The British genius for deception furthered the ruse by passing misinformation through more than a dozen German agents, all of whom had been discovered, arrested, and flipped by British intelligence officers. A network of British double agents with code names such as Garbo and Tricycle embellished the deception, and some 500 false radio reports were sent from London to enemy spymasters in Madrid and thence to Berlin. The Operation Fortitude deception spawned a German hallucination: enemy analysts now detected 79 Allied divisions staging in the United Kingdom, when in fact there were only 52. By late May, Allied intelligence, including Ultra, information gathered through the British ability to intercept and decipher most coded German radio traffic, had uncovered no evidence suggesting "that the enemy has accurately assessed the area in which our main assault is to be made," as Eisenhower learned to his relief. In a final preinvasion fraud, Lieutenant Clifton James of the Royal Army Pay Corps, after spending time studying the many tics of Montgomery, whom he strikingly resembled, flew to Gibraltar on May 26 and then to Algiers. Fitted with a black beret, he strutted about in public for days in hopes that Berlin would conclude that no attack across the channel was imminent if "Monty" was swanning through the Mediterranean.

As May slid toward June, the invasion preparations grew febrile. Every vehicle to be shoved onto the French coast required waterproofing to a depth of 54 inches with a gooey compound of grease, lime, and asbestos fibers and outfitting with a vertical funnel from the exhaust pipe that "stuck up like a wren's tail," to keep the engine from flooding. A single Sherman tank took 300 man-hours to waterproof, occupying a five-man crew for a week. On May 29, Eisenhower also ordered all 11,000 Allied planes to display three broad white stripes on each wing as recognition symbols. A frantic search for 100,000 gallons of whitewash and 20,000 brushes required mobilizing the British paint industry, and workers toiled through the weekend. Some aircrews slathered on the white stripes with push brooms.

Soldiers were provided with seasickness pills, vomit bags, and life belts, incidentals that brought the average rifleman's combat load to 68.4 pounds, far beyond the 43 pounds recommended for assault troops. A company commander in Dorset with the 116th Infantry, bound for Omaha Beach, reported that his men were "loping and braying about the camp under their packs, saying that as long as they were loaded like jackasses they may as well sound like them." On June 2, the men donned "skunk suits," stiff and malodorous uniforms heavily impregnated against poison gas. Each soldier placed his personal effects into a quartermaster box 12 inches long, eight inches wide, and four inches deep, for storage at a depot in Liverpool. Like shedding an old skin or a past life, troops bound for France would fill 500 rail boxcars with such accoutrements of peace every week for the rest of the summer.

"THE TRICK IS TO KEEP MOVING"

Across the fleet, the war cry sounded: "Up anchor!" In the murky, fretful dawn of Monday, June 5, from every English harbor and estuary spilled the great effluent of liberation, from Salcombe and Poole, Dartmouth and Weymouth, in tangled wakes from the Thames past the Black Deep and the Whalebone Marshes, all converging on the white-capped channel: nearly 200,000 seamen and merchant mariners crewing 59 convoys carrying 130,000 soldiers, 2,000 tanks, and 12,000 vehicles.

The early light revealed cutters, corvettes, frigates, freighters, ferries, trawlers, tankers, subchasers: ships for channel marking, cable laying, and smoke making; ships for refrigerating, towing, and hauling food. Leading the fleet was the largest minesweeping operation in naval history. Some 255 vessels began by clearing Area Z, a circular swatch of sea below the Isle of Wight that was ten miles in diameter and soon dubbed Piccadilly Circus. From there, the minesweepers sailed through eight corridors that angled toward a German minefield in the middle of the channel, where a week earlier Royal Navy launches had secretly planted underwater sonic beacons. Electronically dormant until Sunday, the beacons now summoned the sweepers to the entrances of ten channels, each of which was 400 to 1,200 yards wide; these channels would be cleared for 350 miles to five beaches on the Bay of the Seine, in Normandy. Seven-foot waves and a cross-tidal current of nearly three knots bedeviled helmsmen who fought their wheels, the wind, and the sea to keep station. As the sweepers swept, more boats followed to lay a lighted buoy every mile on either side of each channel. The effect, one reporter observed, was "like street lamps across to France."

As the invasion convoys swung toward Area Z, the churlish open English Channel tested the seaworthiness of every landing vessel. The flat-bottomed LST (landing ship, tank) showed what one observer called "a capacity for rolling all ways at once," and the smaller lci (landing craft, infantry) revealed why it was widely derided as a "Lousy Civilian Idea." Worse yet was the LCT (landing craft, tank), capable of only six knots in perfectly calm waters and half that when faced with oncoming waves or currents. Even the U.S. Navy acknowledged that "the LCT is not an ocean-going craft due to poor sea-keeping facilities, low speed, and structural weakness"; the last quality included being bolted together in three sections so that the vessel "gave an ominous impression of being liable to buckle in the middle." Miserable passengers traded seasickness nostrums, such as one sailor's advice to "swallow a pork chop with a string, then pull it up again."

For those who could eat, pork chops were in fact served to the 16th Infantry, with ice cream. Aboard the Thomas Jefferson, 116th Infantry troops ate what one officer described as "bacon and eggs on the edge of eternity." Soldiers primed grenades, sharpened blades, and field-striped their rifles; a U.S. Navy physician recommended that soldiers wash themselves well, sponging away skin bacteria, "in case you stop one." Some Yanks sang "Happy D-Day, dear Adolf, happy D-Day to you," but tommies preferred "Jerusalem," based on William Blake's bitter poem set to music: "Bring me my bow of burning gold." Sailors broke out their battle ensigns, stripped each bridge to fighting trim, and converted mess tables into operating theaters.

To inspirit the men, officers read stand-tall messages from Eisenhower and Montgomery, then offered their own prognostications and advice. "The first six hours will be the toughest," Colonel George Taylor of the 16th Infantry told reporters on the USS Samuel Chase. "They'll just keep throwing stuff onto the beaches until something breaks. That is the plan." Brigadier General Norman Cota told officers aboard the USS Charles Carroll, "You're going to find confusion. The landing craft aren't going in on schedule and people are going to be landed in the wrong place. Some won't be landed at all…. We must improvise, carry on, not lose our heads. Nor must we add to the confusion." A tank battalion commander was more succinct: "The government paid $5 billion for this hour. Get to hell in there and start fighting."

Far inland, at more than a dozen airfields scattered across the United Kingdom, some 20,000 parachutists and glider troops also made ready. Soldiers from the British Sixth Airborne Division blackened their faces with teakettle soot, then chalked bosomy girls and other graffiti on aircraft fuselages while awaiting the order to enplane. "I gave the earth by the runway a good stamp," one private reported.

American paratroopers smeared their skin with cocoa and linseed oil or with charcoal raked from campfires along the taxiways. A few company clowns imitated the singer Al Jolson's minstrel act and joked about the imminent "$10,000 jump" – $10,000 being the maximum death benefit paid by government insurance policies. When a chaplain in the 101st Airborne began to pray aloud, one GI snapped, "I'm not going to die. Cut that crap out." Every man was overburdened, from the burlap strips woven into the helmet net to the knife with a brass-knuckle grip tucked into the jump boots. Also: parachute, reserve chute, life jacket, entrenching tool, rations, fragmentation and smoke grenades, blasting caps, TNT blocks, brass pocket compass, raincoat, blanket, bandoliers, rifle, cigarette carton, and morphine doses ("one for pain and two for eternity"). Carrier pigeons were stuffed into extra GI socks – their heads poking out of little holes cut in the toe – and fastened to paratroopers' jackets. Some officers trimmed the margins from their maps in order to carry a few more rounds of ammunition.

"We look all pockets, pockets and baggy pants. The only visible human parts are two hands," wrote Louis Simpson, the poet who belonged to the 101st Airborne

The Road to D-Day [Excerpt]

Division. "The letter writers are at it again," he continued, "heads bowed over their pens and sheets of paper." Among the scribblers and the map trimmers was the 37-year-old assistant commander of the 82nd Airborne, Brigadier General James Gavin, who confessed in a note to his young daughter, "I have tried to get some sleep this afternoon but to no avail." The impending jump likely would be "about the toughest thing we have tackled," added Gavin, whose exploits in Sicily were among the most storied in the Mediterranean. In his diary, he was more explicit: "Either this 82nd Division job will be the most glorious and spectacular episode in our history or it will be another Little Big Horn. There is no way to tell now.... It will be a very mean and nasty fight."

The prospect of "another Little Big Horn" gnawed at Eisenhower in these final hours. After watching British troops board their lcis from South Parade Pier, in Portsmouth, he sat down to compose a contrite note of responsibility, just in case. "Our landings in the Cherbourg-Havre area have failed to gain a satisfactory foothold and I have withdrawn the troops," he wrote. "If any blame or fault attaches to the attempt it is mine alone." Misdating the paper July 5 – symptomatic of exhaustion and anxiety – he slipped it into his wallet, for use as needed.

Just after 6 PM, Eisenhower climbed into his Cadillac. Leading a three-car convoy, he rolled north for 90 minutes on narrow roads clogged with military trucks. "It's very hard really to look a soldier in the eye when you fear that you are sending him to his death," he told his driver, Kay Summersby. At the Greenham Common airfield, in the Berkshire Downs, outside the eleventh-century town of Newbury, he strolled among the C-47s newly striped with white paint. Troopers with blackened faces and heads shaved or clipped Mohawk style wiggled into their parachute harnesses and sipped a final cup of coffee. "The trick is to keep moving. If you stop, if you start thinking, you lose your focus," Eisenhower told a young soldier from Kansas. "The idea, the perfect idea, is to keep moving."

When he returned to the manor house at his headquarters, in a royal preserve outside London, Eisenhower climbed to the roof to get a final glimpse of his men. "The light of battle was in their eyes," he would write George Marshall, the U.S. Army chief of staff. To Summersby, he confessed, "I hope to God I know what I'm doing."

Red and green navigation lights twinkled across the downs as the sun set at 10:06 PM. Singing voices drifted in the gloaming – "Give me some men who are stout-hearted men / Who will fight for the right they adore" – punctuated by a guttural roar from paratroopers holding their knives aloft in homicidal resolve. Into the airplane bays they heaved themselves, with a helpful shove from behind. Many knelt on the floor to rest their cumbersome gear and chutes on a seat, faces bathed by the soft glow of cigarette embers and red cabin lights. "Give me guts," one trooper prayed. "Give me guts." Engines coughed and caught, the feathered propellers popping as crew chiefs slammed the doors. "Flap your wings, you big-assed bird!" a soldier yelled.

From the west, the last gleam of a dying day glinted off the aluminum fuselages. "Stay, light," a young soldier murmured, "stay on forever, and we'll never get to Normandy."

The light faded and was gone. Deep into the English Channel, 59 darkened convoys went to battle stations as they pushed past the parallel rows of dim buoys: red to starboard, white to port. "This is like trying to slip into a room where everyone is asleep," an officer on the USS Quincy observed.

Small craft struggled in the wind and chop. "Men sick, waves washed over deck," an LCT log recorded. "Stove went out, nothing to eat, explosives wet and could not be dried out." Short seas snapped tow ropes, flooded engine rooms, and sloshed through troop compartments. Some helmsmen held their wheels 30 degrees off true to keep course. Several heaving vessels blinked a one-word message: "Seasick. Seasick. Seasick."

Down the ten channels they plunged, two designated for each of the five forces steaming toward the five beaches to which planners had given the code names Utah, Omaha, Gold, Juno, and Sword. Wakes braided and rebraided. The amber orb of a full moon rose through a thinning overcast off the port bow, and the sea sang as swells slipped along every hull bound for a better world. Hallelujah, sang the sea. Hallelujah. Hallelujah.∂ [Full Article]

RICK ATKINSON is an author and military historian. His most recent book is *The Guns at Last Light: The War in Western Europe, 1944-1945* (Henry Holt, 2013), from which this essay is adapted. Copyright © 2013 by Rick Atkinson. Reprinted by arrangement with Henry Holt and Company, LLC. All rights reserved.

© Foreign Affairs

October 1944

America at War: The End Begins [Excerpt]

Hanson W. Baldwin

REUTERS

IN the summer of 1944 the American Army came of age. The successful invasion of Normandy and the quick capture of Cherbourg in June meant the negation, in a strategic sense, of all Hitler's hopes and marked the beginning of the end for Germany. In rapid succession, in late July and August, the forces of the Allies broke out from the Cotentin peninsula, smashed much of the German Seventh Army, overran Brittany, captured Paris and reached the Meuse at Sedan. Simultaneously, they invaded southern France. Coupled with great German defeats on the Eastern Front, the defections in the Balkans and convulsions within the Nazi Reich, these victories put the unmistakable stamp of success on an American "amateur army," raised, organized, trained and equipped within five years.

The summer of 1944 was also a season of American triumphs in the Pacific. The conquest of the Marianas was almost as important a milestone in the history of the

Pacific war as the invasion of France was in the European struggle. In the South Pacific, the advances in New Guinea put our forces on the doorstep of the Philippines; and in Burma, despite the monsoon, British, American and Chinese forces won remarkable and still growing victories.

The reactions expressed in Germany in the machinations of the Hitler "assassination plot," and in Japan by the fall of the Tojo cabinet, were direct reflections of the Allied successes. Both in the East and the West the end was beginning to be clearly defined.

II

The invasion of western Europe was the greatest and most successful combined operation of its type in military history. Some 8,000 Allied planes gave direct or indirect support to the landings, and 800 fighting craft, ranging in size from trawlers and motor torpedo boats to 16-inch gunned battleships, supported an invasion fleet of more than 3,200 transports and landing craft. The initial airborne operations involved the landing of three divisions by parachute and glider, probably the greatest airborne operation ever undertaken. In sheer magnitude, there has been nothing in the history of amphibious operations to compare with the Normandy invasion.

Some of the superlatives applied to it have been exaggerated, however. Far larger and more modern fighting fleets than the Anglo-American task forces that steamed across the Channel have operated in the Pacific. Many of the techniques of amphibious war in the Pacific are more advanced than those applied in the Bay of the Seine; indeed, our whole magnificent concept of amphibious war and combined operations is a product of our Pacific experience. Some of the weapons used in the early fighting in France were not as new or effective as those this correspondent has seen in other theaters and in the United States. Despite some pre-D-Day misgivings of this and other observers, nevertheless, the forces and weapons employed proved to be more than adequate for the job; the first stage of the invasion was far easier, and Allied casualties far lighter, than had been expected.

German opposition was not so strong as foreseen. In retrospect, it appears certain that the removal of Marshal von Rundstedt, the German commander in France at the time of the invasion, was for cause; he had had two years to strengthen the defenses of the French coast, and yet until Marshal Erwin Rommel's inspection in the winter of 1943-44 many obvious measures of defense were not taken. At the time of the invasion, the beach and coast defenses had been considerably improved since the winter, and troops had been shifted to the Normandy region. Fortifications were still in progress; in one 500-yard strip of beach this correspondent saw three heavy reënforced concrete casemates still under construction, and in numerous pastures "Rommel's asparagus" – heavy wooden posts up-ended in the earth to prevent airborne landings – were in course of installation.

The German defenses, though formidable, were not so dense on D-Day as the Japanese obstacles encountered at Tarawa or in the Marshalls, in the opinion of this correspondent and of officers who had served in the Pacific. But in the Pacific we had never assaulted a continental land mass, or a beach dominated by high cliffs, as we did in one landing in Normandy. So far, the Japanese opportunity for counteroffensive has been limited, since our naval and air superiority has enabled us to cut the sea-lanes by which Japanese insular positions could receive reënforcements. In Europe we attacked a continent and faced the danger that the enemy's land-based lines of communication might give him a chance to smash our beachheads. His inability to launch that large-scale counteroffensive which was so much feared prior to D-Day has been due to the same factors of sea and air superiority that have won us success in the Pacific; of course it was also a result of the great Russian offensive, which so threatened the German position that the process of shifting troops from east to west, actually begun in June, had to be halted and reversed.

The victories of D-Day and the immediate weeks thereafter had their antecedents, therefore, in the months of bitter struggle that broke the back of the German submarine campaign, and in the great air battles that raged over the Reich in 1943 and 1944. Perhaps the most significant date in the history of the air war is the week of February 20-26, 1944, when the great bombers of the Eighth Air Force dealt a well-nigh mortal blow to the German aircraft industry. The limited scale of German air opposition in June of 1944 gave it pregnant meaning. The pre-invasion bombings not only defeated the Luftwaffe, but smashed so heavily at German land communications that the enemy's ability to reënforce and supply his divisions in Normandy was greatly impaired. And after D-Day we dominated the daytime skies so completely that the vaunted power of the German Army to manœuvre was also greatly weakened.... [Full Article]

HANSON W. BALDWIN, military and naval correspondent of the New York Times; author of "The Caissons Roll," "Strategy for Victory" and other works

© Foreign Affairs

July 1945

America at War: Victory in Europe [Excerpt]

Hanson W. Baldwin

MINISTRY OF INFORMATION PHOTO DIVISION PHOTOGRAPHER / WIKIMEDIA COMMONS

V-E Day Celebrations in London, May 8, 1945.

NAPOLEON'S remark that the "moral is to the physical as three to one" again received the affirmation of history in the spring of 1945 when German resistance collapsed suddenly and the war in Europe ended after five years and eight months of unprecedented struggle.

The exact date of the ending of the war against Germany may long be a matter of debate among historians. The first surrender agreement was signed at Reims, France, on May 7; this was "countersigned" in Berlin May 8-9, and all hostilities were scheduled to end 12:01 a.m. May 9. Actually some German troops were still fighting the Russians on May 13. But for all intents and purposes the war ended in April with the great American sweep to the Elbe and the Russian drive into Berlin.

America at War: Victory in Europe [Excerpt]

At that time, there seemed a real possibility that the German resistance in pockets throughout Europe from the Ægean Islands to Norway might be bitter and perhaps protracted; indeed, this was expected, for high SHAEF officials had told correspondents that the "campaign of the pockets" might continue throughout the summer. German fanaticism and will to fight had already extended the war – despite the hopelessness of the German position and the tremendous superiority of the Allies – long beyond the expected ending. In the spring of 1945, then, the Allies tended to be justifiably cautious in their predictions. But the sweep to the Elbe, the drive into Berlin, and, above all, the Nazi announcement of Adolf Hitler's death on May 1 snapped the thread of German morale. Wholesale surrenders were also touched off by the Nazi collapse in Italy. The "campaign of the pockets" was never fought.

The announcement of Hitler's death seems to have been coupled with the assumption of power by the German military. But that did not end the power of the Nazi Party. The Nazi announcement was that Hitler had died in the Berlin Chancellery, then under attack by the Russians. Hitler probably is dead, though no proof of this may ever be available. We may never know how he died. All this is as expected, and contributes materially to the "Hitler myth," which – unless we are careful – may become part and parcel of German folk history. Hitler is not "dead" and will not be as long as his spirit roams the world.

At long last, therefore, another conqueror's attempt to dominate the entire Continent of Europe has been blocked, and the dangerous philosophy that the end justifies any means has again been invalidated by the indignation of the peoples of the earth. The war against Hitler was perhaps the most successful coalition war of modern times, and the coördination between the war efforts of the United States and the British Empire was better than in any previous great war by allies. Two tremendous factors operated to bring about Germany's defeat: British courage in adversity, when "the few" of the air turned back "the many"; and Russian manpower and the vastness of Russian distances. But the cornerstone of victory was the American machine. The mass industrial output of America provided the sinews of conflict for all the Allies. Without it victory would have been impossible and Germany's will to fight would never have been undermined and her armies defeated.

The war ended with Germany perhaps the most devastated and thoroughly beaten nation since Carthage. But it was a costly victory. The United States alone suffered more than 800,000 casualties, including more than 155,000 killed. Alone it spent between 150 and 200 billion dollars. And Europe, in the guise man had known it in modern times, was gone forever.

"Victory" is an unsatisfactory term so long as we are faced with the problems that the physical struggle left in its wake. They are gigantic, far more complex than those of battle. Politically and economically, morally and psychologically, Europe is a wasted land. Even that stark reality, however, is no guarantee that the ravening urge for dominion of men over other men has ended; even before the fires of war had died, there were disquieting signs in eastern Europe and in the Balkans that the "self-determination of peoples" might be merely a phrase. The rejoicing on V-E Day, therefore, was tempered throughout the United States by the awareness of the immense difficulties that remain, by the fear of our people that the "Four Horsemen" may again ride through Europe, and particularly by the knowledge that there is still a war – tremendous in its dimensions – to be won in the Pacific.

II

The final defeat of Germany is seen in retrospect to have been clearly a product of the Allied invasion of western Europe. Whether Germany could have been defeated without that invasion is problematical; in any case the war would certainly have lasted far longer. The invasion in the west, the sweep across France, the drive to the Westwall, the attrition struggle along that fortified zone, the push to the Rhine, the drive across, and the capture of the Saar and the Ruhr stretched German resistance to the breaking-point.

The fruits of these operations were immense – about 2,100,000 German prisoners in the west from D-Day, June 6, 1944, until the end of fighting in the Ruhr pocket, April 19, 1945 – plus the unreckoned total of German killed, wounded and missing. In that period, too, the Allied advances were so important that Germany's strategical position became hopeless; she had been deprived of most of her industrial areas; she no longer possessed strategic barriers or a continuous line in the west; and our intensive bombings had crippled the mobility of the German Army and was bleeding the Third Reich white.

The direct antecedents of the final campaigns against Germany go back to the "Battle of the Bulge" in December and January, when in the bitter Ardennes winter the last great German blow in the west was beaten back. We now know from the statements of the captured German commander at the time, Field Marshal von Rundstedt, that the Nazi objective was to relieve Allied pressure in the Cologne Plain area, and if possible to reach Liege and the line of the Meuse, thus disrupting many of the Allied supply lines through Belgium. This offensive failed in its maximum objective, but succeeded in its minimum one – to relieve the Cologne pressure and to win time. But the German successes, which were temporary, were immediately imperiled by the great Russian offensive of January, which swept from the Vistula to the Oder. The Germans drew some 20 divisions away from the western front to reënforce the east. At the same time, we belatedly strained every nerve to give our ground forces that ratio of superiority which is essential if battles are to be won. We sent to Europe at least two divisions that had been earmarked for the Pacific, and hurriedly built up the strength of our ground army in the west. The last new division to reach Europe entered the fighting only a month before the end.

The marked weakening of the German forces, the marked strengthening of our own, plus the better weather of February, March and April which permitted us to use our air superiority to the full, explain in some measure the rapidity of our final successes. But good leadership and flexible tactics, plus the skill and determination of the American Army, contributed materially to victory; the Army of Europe ended its career of blood and glory the best fighting machine the United States ever has sent abroad.

The final campaign in Germany was prefaced by the fighting in February west of the Rhine. The capture of the dams controlling the level of the Roer River by the First Army did not come in time to prevent flooding of that valley by the retreating Germans. As a result, the Ninth Army offensive across the Roer toward Düsseldorf and Muenchen-Gladbach, originally timed to coincide with the Canadian and British drive toward Cleve and Emmerich, had to be delayed until late February. When it started, however, on February 23, it went with a rush. The Ninth Army, despite the flood waters in the Roer, spanned that river rapidly and drove northwest to meet the British and Canadians coming down from the north. The junction was soon made, and by March 6 the Ninth Army – operating at the time as part of Field Marshal Sir Bernard L. Montgomery's Twenty-first Army Group – had reached the Rhine, except in the north, where German paratroopers tenaciously held a bridgehead on the west bank at Wesel.

Enemy casualties for this part of the operation alone totalled about 52,000 captured (for the Twenty-first Army Group) and an estimated 60,000 killed and wounded. Simultaneous with the Ninth Army's crossing of the Roer, the First American Army – "workhorse" of the American armies in Europe – drove eastward toward Cologne and Bonn. It then turned southeastward to join spearheads with the Third American Army, which had sent its "galloping" tanks of the famous 4th Armored Division on a deep drive from the captured road junction of Pruem into Coblenz.

Then occurred one of those historic incidents which, though it did not change the course of the war, perhaps shortened it and surely lessened our casualties. The 9th Armored Division of the First Army reached a railroad bridge across the Rhine at Remagen after the Germans had damaged it but before they could destroy it. A platoon leader alive to his opportunities sent his men across and was quickly followed by other forces. On General of the Army Dwight D. Eisenhower's personal orders, Lieutenant-General Courtney Hodges of the First Army hurriedly pushed at least five divisions over the Rhine, and by March 24 we had a firm, deep and wide bridgehead on the east bank. The Remagen bridge subsequently collapsed from cumulative damage, but as Lieutenant-General Walter B. Smith, General Eisenhower's chief of staff, said, "It did not last long, but while it did it was worth its weight in gold."

While the First Army was developing and expanding its bridgehead and clearing out pockets along its front west of the Rhine, General George C. Patton's Third Army seized Coblenz and cleaned out German troops west of the Moselle River. It then crossed the Moselle at several points (two of the principal crossings were south of Coblenz and near Trier) and drove southeast toward Mannheim to cut off the Saar and the German forces defending it. At the same time, the Seventh American Army, Lieutenant-General Alexander Patch commanding, drove through the Westwall defenses in the Saar and acted as the anvil to the First Army's hammer. These converging operations badly mauled the German First and Seventh Armies, netted great bags of prisoners and equipment, and completed the rout of the enemy west of the Rhine. At the same time, the Wesel bridgehead in the north was wiped out by the Twenty-first Army Group after tough fighting, and by March 24, one month after the Roer crossing, all German positions west of the Rhine (except for a small bridgehead west of Karlsruhe) had been liquidated. A considerable number of German troops escaped to the east bank, however. When the effort to break across the river started on March 24, the Allies were faced by the remnants of perhaps seven German armies, among them the Twenty-fifth Army, First Parachute Army, Fifteenth Army, Fifth Panzer Army, Seventh Army, First Army and Nineteenth Army. But this was a more impressive list on paper than in action; we probably enjoyed a superiority in combat effectives of between two and three to one.

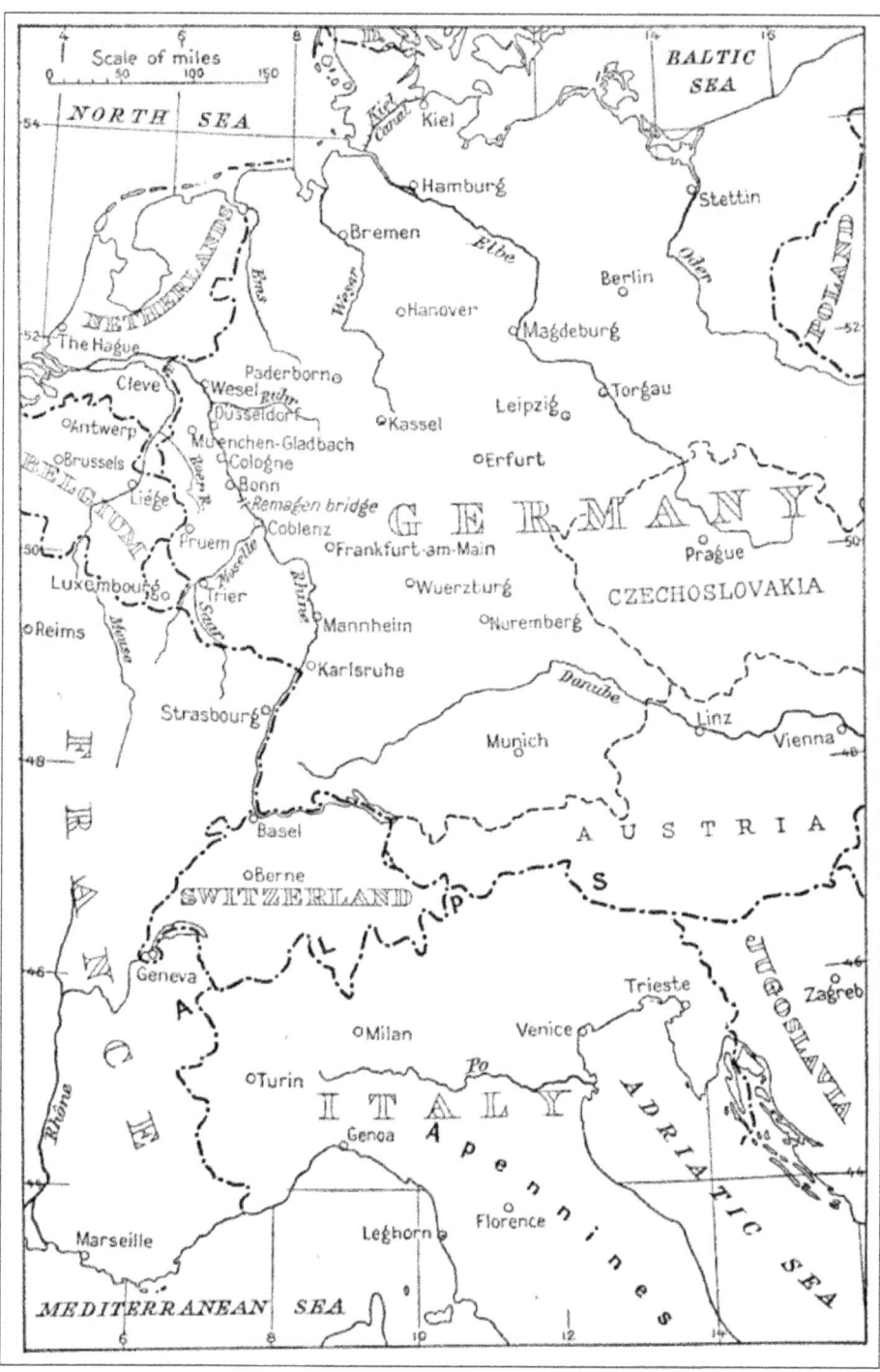

The great value of the Remagen bridgehead now showed itself. The strategical mobility of the German Army was greatly reduced, and at this period its tactical mobility was terrifically impaired by our well-planned interdiction bombing: it was exceedingly difficult for the Germans to shift what few reserves they had. The Remagen bridgehead had forced them to weaken their forces in the north, opposite Field Marshal Montgomery's Twenty-first Army Group, and they had built up a strong front on the east bank of the Rhine south of Cologne to protect the Ruhr. But instead of striking due north from the bridgehead through the heavily built-up areas of the Ruhr, the First Army struck south to connect up with the Third near Frankfurt-am-Main, and then east and north to encircle the Ruhr. The advance out of the Remagen bridgehead was accompanied by a general crossing of the Rhine along most of its length from Arnhem to Karlsruhe. The main effort originally had been scheduled for the favorable terrain of the Westphalian Plain in the north, where Field Marshal Montgomery's First Canadian and Second British Armies, reënforced by the Ninth American Army, had been expected to make the main Rhine crossing. The Germans correctly diagnosed this as a point of danger, but apparently did not expect – or did not have enough reserves to meet – the eastward lunge of the First Army and the crossing of the Rhine by the Third Army north of Mannheim.

The British crossings in the north, aided and eased by naval landing craft, and by troops of the U. S. 17th Airborne Division and British paratroopers of the First Allied Airborne Army who were landed in the enemy's rear after the ground troops had started their offensive, were made with remarkable ease. It soon became evident that the Rhine was too lightly defended, the German Army's mobility too greatly circumscribed, for the river to be made an effective barrier. By April 8 the battle of the Rhine was a memory; the American Ninth and the British Second in the north had crossed the Ems and the Weser Rivers; the Third had crossed the Weser in the south; the Seventh Army was past Wuerzburg; and the French First Army had crossed the Rhine north of Karlsruhe.

More important, the First Army and the Ninth Army had linked at Paderborn, so that the Ruhr, last of Germany's great industrial areas, was encircled. This, like the forging of the Remagen bridgehead, was a decisive stroke. General Smith called the Ruhr encirclement the "largest double envelopment of military history," and while this may be a slight exaggeration, it was certainly the greatest single pocket ever created by American troops. Some 317,000 Germans were captured by April 19, when the Ruhr pocket was finally wiped out, and the greater part of two to three German armies were destroyed. From then on, there was never a continuous front in the west: the fighting was fluid, a battle of "pockets" against isolated German elements, some dispirited, some fanatical.

The Ninth Army rejoined General Omar Bradley's Twelfth Army Group after the Ruhr encirclement. With the Ninth, First, Third and Fifteenth Armies [ii] under his command in the last phase of the war against Germany, General Bradley controlled the greatest field force ever led by an American general. The First and Ninth, after cleaning up the Ruhr, drove northeastward deep into Germany, while the British and Canadians turned to the north against the German ports. The Ninth reached the Elbe near Magdeburg on April 11, and pushed one bridgehead across the river north of the city. This bridgehead was smashed by a German counterattack, but another bridgehead was made good and was being developed when General Eisenhower ordered the Ninth and First Armies to halt along the Elbe and await the advancing Russians.

This decision probably was not made at the Yalta Conference, and may have been taken by General Eisenhower as a result of the field situation. The Russians had started a push from their Oder positions in late April, shortly before we reached the Elbe. They unquestionably wished the prestige of entering Berlin first. The communication lines of the First and Ninth Armies were extended and supplies were being delivered by air; only weak spearheads had crossed the Elbe, and the Germans had sizeable forces east of that river. Moreover, even though the supply difficulties could have been solved in a few days – considering the disorganized state of German resistance – a continued Allied push into the corridor between the Elbe and the Oder would have risked a head-on meeting with the Russians, mistakes in identifications of units, and possible casualties and incidents. And an Allied attempt to take Berlin from the west would have complicated the siege, for we have never had any coördinated command with the Russians. Probably it would have cost the Americans very heavily in casualties. This last factor doubtless was a governing one in General Eisenhower's decision.

Juncture with the Russians was made near Torgau by units of the First American Army on April 25, to the accompaniment of much vodka drinking and wassail, and Germany was split in half. Meanwhile, the Third American Army, which captured Frankfurt after crossing the Rhine and formed a juncture with the right flank of the First, pushed to the northeast toward Kassel and Erfurt. It reached the border of Czechoslovakia on April 18; then this powerful army swung abruptly 90 degrees to the southeast and joined the American Seventh – which had been fighting through Nuremberg against bitter resistance – and the French First, in a drive to smash the German southern citadel.

How long the Germans in this region, as well as those in Norway and in other pockets throughout Europe, could have held out we shall never know. For from April 21 on, when the Russians first entered Berlin, events moved fast. The Russians had captured Vienna on April 13, and our great victories in the west had paved the way for the final curtain. The collapse started in Italy. On May 2 the Allied High Command there announced the unconditional surrender – signed April 29, after a long period of negotiations – of all Nazi and Italian Fascist forces in Italy. The capitulation followed a blitz campaign of less than a month, in which the weary veterans of the Apennines came down at last out of the mountains into the "promised land" of the Po Valley and swept on northward to the Alps. The surrender in Italy exposed the southern flank of the so-called Nazi redoubt.

But even before the surrender was announced more important events had occurred. The death of Adolf Hitler in Berlin was broadcast by the Nazi radio on May 1, and Grand Admiral Karl Doenitz, plainly named to execute the capitulation, took over. Every soldier of the Third Reich had been sworn to personal loyalty to Hitler, and the whole Army was "inspired" by one man as few armies have been since Napoleon's Grand Army. Hitler's disappearance released the German troops from the oath of fealty; the house of cards collapsed. While negotiations with the Doenitz régime went on, forces in the field surrendered piecemeal in the west – first the Germans in northern Germany and Denmark, then those in Holland, then those in southern Germany and Austria. The end came in the dark of the morning at Reims: one of the German representatives wept, but another – Colonel-General Jodl, haughty to the last – demanded that the German people be treated "with generosity."

So the curtain fell in Europe on the greatest tragedy in the history of that old and weary Continent. As it fell, the spotlight of history was playing upon some 67 American divisions, the greatest army ever sent across any sea…. [Full Article]

HANSON W. BALDWIN, military and naval correspondent of the New York Times; author of "The Caissons Roll," "Strategy for Victory" and other works

© Foreign Affairs

October 1945

America at War: Victory in the Pacific [Excerpt]

Hanson W. Baldwin

USS Bunker Hill hit by two Kamikazes

AUGUST 6, 1945, will remain forever a milestone in human annals. On that date the world's first atomic fission bomb was dropped upon Japan. The action may have been necessary for the purpose of saving American lives. But it was not merely another episode in the long history of man's inhumanity to man; and it was even more portentous than the final victory over Japan which quickly followed. For it marked the first harnessing of the sun's power on a large scale, with all the untold consequences for good and evil implicit in the achievement. The new chapter may end in man's reversion to a troglodyte, or it may lead to the establishment of a world brotherhood in which the forces of nature, including man's own passions, are harnessed to the common good.

II

The war against Japan reached its end as suddenly as it had begun, months before most of our military leaders had dared to hope for it. The surprise ending was a consequence of the atomic bombing of Hiroshima and Nagasaki and of Russia's eleventh-hour entry into the conflict, but it was also a result of our previous sweeping victories in the Pacific. Even before August 6, Japan was hopelessly beaten. The only unresolved question was whether she would continue a futile struggle and make us pay still further in lives and time, or whether her leaders would accept the inevitable and bow in defeat. The atomic bomb speeded their decision; but the strategic situation in the Pacific, especially our capture of Iwo Jima and Okinawa, which unlocked the gateways to Japan, was a decisive factor. Significantly, the first Japanese peace overtures were made to Russia about the time the campaign on Okinawa ended.

The conquest of Okinawa was one of the most dearly-bought of American triumphs. It was not only a land victory, but the greatest and most protracted battle of ships against planes in history. The campaign started well. One Army and one Marine Corps, organized as the Tenth Army under Lieutenant-General Simon Bolivar Buckner, Jr., landed virtually unopposed on the western "waist" of Okinawa on April 1. The Marines turned north and quickly mopped up their sector of the island, but the Army divisions encountered major resistance along the so-called Naha-Shuri line. This fortified line extended across the island north of the capital, Naha, and took advantage of the ramparts of the ancient castle of Shuri and of all defensive features of the terrain. The assault bogged down to a fierce step-by-step advance which cost us heavy casualties.

The Japanese strategy then became apparent. Our troops on the island were struggling against a fanatic enemy, in hilly, difficult country, amidst, at times, torrential rains. The Japanese Kamikaze, or suicide fliers, who had made their first appearance in force in the Philippine campaign, now attacked our fleet, which was supporting our beachhead. Day after day and night after night, the enemy threw his air power against our sea power. The significance of this struggle largely escaped the American people; but it actually counted for more in settling the fate of Okinawa, and eventually of Japan, than did the fighting on land. Our ships were the key to our operations in the Pacific. They maintained the indispensable supply link which enabled the ground soldiers to operate. The support of naval aircraft from carrier decks, of naval gunfire and of naval landing craft was essential to victory.

The fleet was committed to action in a restricted area within easy reach of the enemy's land bases. The Japanese always knew where to find it, because – if it were to fulfill its mission – it had to be in close proximity to the American-held portion of Okinawa. The resulting struggle between our "C.A.P." (combat air patrol) and our surface ships and the Japanese Kamikaze fliers went on, in some periods continuously, for almost three months. In a single day the Japanese made hundreds of attacks, of which our radar picket line of light craft bore the brunt. Hundreds of Japanese planes were shot down. Many of our destroyers were sunk or damaged, and some larger ships were also put out of action. Significantly, in the Okinawa campaign more men were killed in the Navy than in the Army or the Marine Corps. Indeed, Okinawa was the most expensive single campaign in our naval history. When the smoke had cleared, however, it was seen that "the fleet that came to stay" had defeated the suicide fliers. In retrospect, it is apparent that a decision in the whole struggle against Japan had been reached.

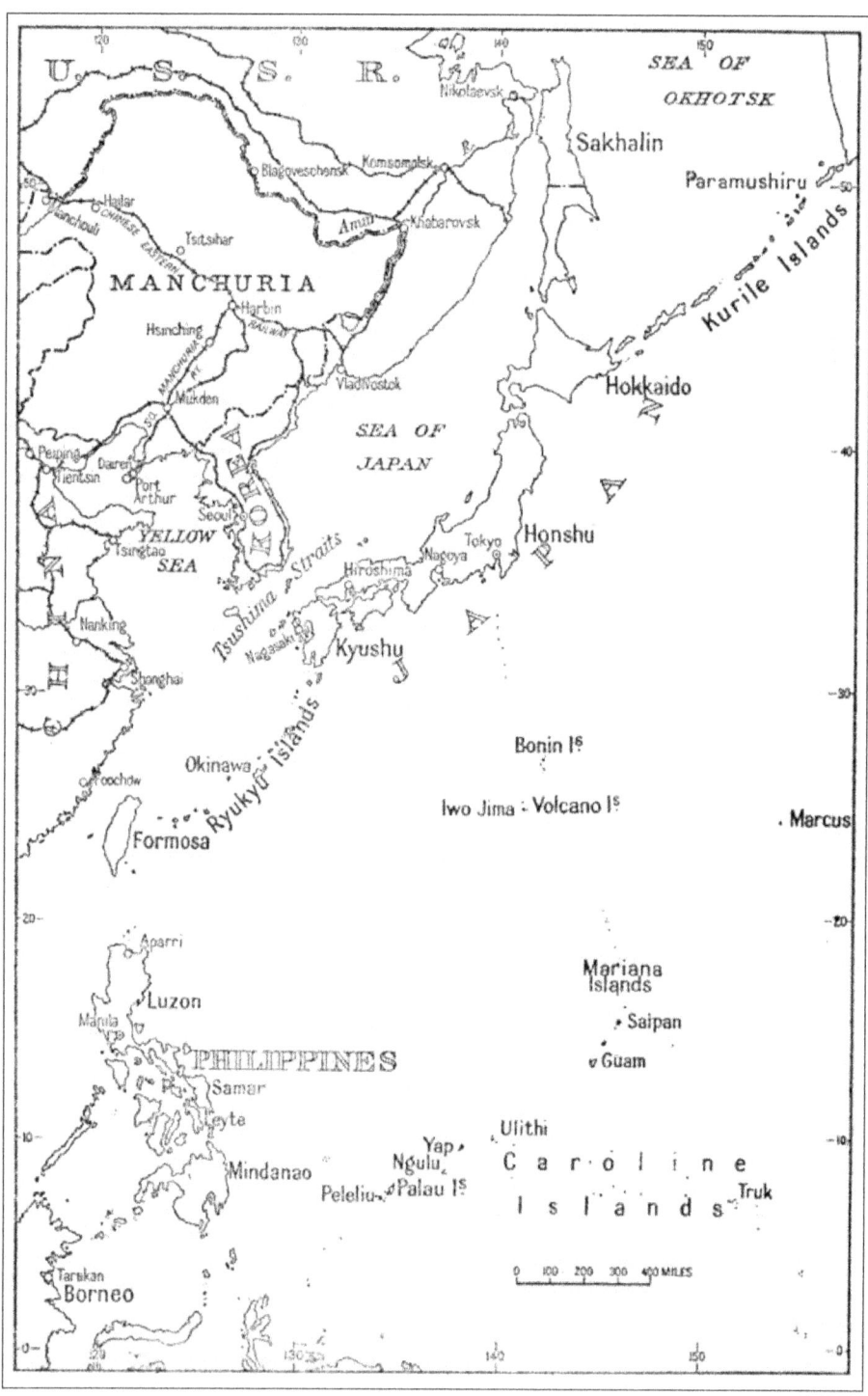

The fighting on the island itself proved to be no less exacting.

The Naha-Shuri line was one of the best-defended positions that American troops have been called on to attack in this war. The Japanese fought with tenacity and skill. The Third Marine Amphibious Corps, after mopping up the northern part of the island, wheeled into line beside the Twenty-fourth (Army) Corps, so that at times four and five divisions were attacking the enemy simultaneously. Even with this addition to our strength the going continued hard and costly. Near the end of the campaign, the 8th Marine Regimental combat team – fresh troops of the 2nd Marine Division – "sparked" the final clean-up. The island was declared to be securely in our hands on June 21. Enemy casualties were estimated at 118,000, including some 10,000 prisoners. Our own casualties were heavy: Army, 3,761 killed, 14,415 wounded, and 236 missing; Navy, 4,907 killed and missing, 4,824 wounded; Marines, 2,573 killed and missing, 12,565 wounded.

The Okinawa campaign was fought soundly, if not brilliantly. We made some mistakes. Our original intelligence estimates of enemy strength were too low. After the success of our early landings, the 2nd Marine Division, which had been in floating reserve, was sent back to rear area bases, and none of its elements was used until the final phase. No attempt was made to outflank the enemy by sea, admittedly a difficult operation. Finally, our tanks – as in Europe – were not sufficiently armored and in some instances were not well handled.

The loss of Okinawa persuaded the Japanese to make their first definite peace approaches, through Moscow. Had the war continued, the island would have proved, in our hands, the key to the Japanese main islands.

During and after the fighting on Okinawa we continued our large-scale mopping-up operations in the Philippines. Troops of the Sixth Army (General Walter Krueger) and the Eighth Army (Lieutenant-General Robert L. Eichelberger) attacked the Japanese positions in Luzon and concentrations in the jungles of Mindanao. After the enemy was routed out of an intricate system of caves astride the Manila water supply region, the principal fighting on Luzon took place in the Cagayan Valley and the surrounding rugged hills. Here, the Japanese commander-in-chief in the Philippines, General Tomoyuki Yamashita, made his last stand with a sizeable body of troops. On Mindanao, the fighting in uncharted jungles dragged on well into the summer.

By July 5, however, General Douglas MacArthur was able to announce that the "Philippine Islands are now liberated and the … campaigns can be regarded as virtually closed." He estimated that the enemy had employed the equivalent of 23 divisions, and that about 450,000 Japanese had been killed, captured or dispersed. These figures are far higher than the estimates of Japanese strength in the Philippines made before the invasion began, and they probably include Filipino collaborationists. Though we employed only 17 divisions in the campaign, we always were able to oppose superior forces to the enemy because the Japanese were scattered throughout the archipelago; further, our naval and air superiority gave us additional mobility and power. American Army casualties for the entire campaign up to July 7 were 12,035 killed, 1,196 missing and 46,425 wounded. These do not include Navy or Marine casualties. As the war closed, the 38th Division was still mopping up the enemy in the watershed area east of Manila; the 32nd was still tracking down the enemy in the hills of northern Luzon; and the 31st was operating in Mindanao.

The Philippines campaign was the greatest single land campaign of the Pacific. Our casualties, however, were remarkably light. As in the case of our other Pacific victories, our success depended upon our control of the sea; our sea power made our victory certain. On the whole, the campaign was well led and well fought....

III

Simultaneously with these great land operations, great naval and air campaigns were under way against Japan proper. The attack was launched on July 10 by the Third Fleet, under Admiral William F. Halsey, Jr., and was interrupted only by the end of the war. So sustained and so effective was this attack that it broke all precedents in the annals of naval war. First the area of the Tokyo plain was hit by planes. On July 14 this blow was followed by another against northern Honshu and by the first surface-ship bombardment of the main Japanese islands. Then, in quick succession – sometimes with intervals of only one day – the Fleet struck again and again with planes and with the guns of surface ships against widely separated objectives on Hokkaido and Honshu.

The American sea forces thus engaged comprised nine battleships, 16 carriers, 19 cruisers and 62 destroyers. This tremendous sea force was reënforced on July 17 by one British battleship, four British carriers, six British cruisers and 17 British destroyers. The combined fleets put some 1,500 planes into the air. During the 37 days the operations lasted, the ships never once dropped anchor and practically never stopped their engines. They were refueled, reammunitioned, and resupplied at sea by the greatest service force of tankers, ammunition ships and supply ships the world has ever seen.

In the last two-and-a-half months of the war (including those epic final 37 days) the Third Fleet wreaked almost incredible destruction in its various attacks on Japan proper as well as on islands in the Okinawa area and on outlying Japanese bases. The enemy offered very light resistance in the air. This was in part the result of a shortage of gasoline, spare parts and trained pilots, in part of a deliberate attempt to conserve planes against the day of our expected invasion. Only an estimated 290 enemy planes were shot down in combat; but more than 1,300 were destroyed on the ground, and another 1,300 were damaged. In all, 48 enemy warships, ranging in size from battleships to landing craft, were sunk and 100 more were damaged. An estimated 529 merchant vessels of all sizes from big freighters to coastal luggers were sunk and almost 1,000 damaged. Major destruction was visited upon factories, industrial areas and airfields. Even if allowance is made for exuberant exaggeration, these figures still are startling; they show how weak Japan really was in the last phase of the war. Japanese ineffectiveness becomes particularly clear when these losses are measured against our own extremely light ones. In the final five weeks, not a single ship of the Third Fleet was sunk, and only one was lightly damaged.[iii]

But for men of the United States Navy on every sea the peak of satisfaction was derived from the great two-day raids made by Halsey's carriers against Japan's naval dockyards on the Inland Sea in late July. These raids sank or damaged about 20 Japanese men-of-war and left the remnants of the Japanese Fleet broken and burning. When the smoke cleared away, the Japanese Navy had perhaps one battleship, the Nagato, still afloat but damaged, two aircraft carriers still afloat but damaged, and a handful of cruisers, destroyers and submarines. Such was the end, in the Inland Sea, far from open water, of what had once been the world's third largest fleet. Pearl Harbor was avenged.

While the Third Fleet was continuing to strike Japan with all its tremendous power, small surface units and planes several times reconnoitered and attacked the Kurile Islands north of Japan and even penetrated into the Sea of Okhotsk. Further south in the Pacific, the enemy-held islands which had been by-passed were attacked regularly by air and occasionally by sea. These attacks kept them thoroughly neutralized, and at the last some of the enemy garrisons – notably that on Wake – began to run short of food.

In addition to these great undertakings, the Navy's Fleet Air Wings, aided by submarines, instituted far-flung blockade operations which in the final phases of the war penetrated the Sea of Japan. Land planes and flying boats, operating from the Ryukyus and the Marianas, swept the East China Sea and the Yellow Sea practically clean of enemy shipping. They made long patrols daily over the coast of China from Formosa to Tsushima, and even penetrated inland and attacked Japanese land communications on the Asiatic mainland. Most important in the blockade, however, was the partial severance of the enemy's lifeline across the Straits of Tsushima. Probably the route was never completely closed, but the waters became hazardous for enemy shipping.

The blockade was aided greatly by the laying of mines, chiefly by the B-29 Superfortresses of the Twentieth Air Force. The Navy planned this campaign, furnished the mines and trained the Twentieth Air Force in their use. Beginning in the spring of 1945, the big bombers laid mines regularly – even in the Inland Sea and Korean ports. In all, more than 12,000 mines were laid in 45 different areas. It was probably the greatest aerial minelaying operation in the history of war.

But perhaps the most effective operations of the last months of the war – certainly the most spectacular – were the great assaults upon Japanese cities conducted by our giant Superfortresses based in the Marianas. Between November 24, 1944, and the end of hostilities the B-29's flew 32,612 sorties in 318 missions and dropped 169,421 tons of bombs and mines on about 64 Japanese urban industrial areas, 85 industrial plants, 102 airfields, one railway yard, and various harbor and coastal areas. The first attacks, made at extremely high altitudes with high explosive bombs, were not particularly successful. Major-General Curtis E. LeMay, probably the foremost bomber commander of this war, then sent his planes in at startlingly low levels –5,000 to 10,000 feet – using jellied petroleum incendiary bombs. These attacks burned out an estimated 158 square miles of Japanese cities and left an estimated 8,480,000 persons homeless or dead. Tokyo, attacked six times in massive fire raids, was more than 50 percent destroyed, and an average of 39.5 percent of all cities attacked were burned out.[iv] These massive attacks cost us (from November 24, 1944) a total of 437 combat losses of the B-29's; probably a greater number were lost from operational accidents. The toll in men was 3,267. About 600 men were picked up by rescue planes or naval vessels.

These tremendous strategic air assaults, which were intended to soften up the enemy, would have been greatly intensified after Lieutenant-General James H. Doolittle's Eighth Air Force of Superfortresses, based on Okinawa, joined in the attack. The Eighth Air Force, redeployed at least in name from Europe, was about ready to start operations when the war ended. After the capture of Okinawa, the strategical bombing of the "heavies" was complemented by tactical attacks upon Japanese cities, docks, industries and communications by elements of the Fifth, Seventh and Thirteenth Air Forces, all part of the Far East Air Forces of General George C. Kenney, General MacArthur's air commander. These strikes, too, had still to reach their peak when the war ended.

Japan, then, was subjected during June, July and early August to the gathering might of one of the most tremendous air assaults ever launched against a nation – strategic mass attacks by the B-29's and tactical attacks upon specific targets by carrier aircraft of the Fleet and by the land-based fighters, medium bombers, and four-engined "light-heavies" based on Okinawa and Iwo, plus the blockade operations by the Navy's Fleet Air Wings and aerial mining. There is no doubt that even by the middle of July Japan was in a much weakened state. Her air and maritime power were dwindling and some of her raw material shortages were. becoming serious.

To Japan's other troubles were added major troubles in China and southeast Asia. Early in the summer it became apparent that the British Southeast Asia Command was preparing (with considerable American supply help and some staff assistance) an assault upon Malaya as soon as the monsoon season was over, with Singapore as the objective. In the spring the Japanese had been forced to begin withdrawing men from parts of China in order to provide more troops for their "inner defense zone" – the main Japanese islands, Korea, Manchuria and north China. This movement now became pronounced. China's fighting strength meanwhile increased steadily as supplies poured in by air "over the Hump" and by the Stilwell Road. The Chinese Combat Command, reorganized by Lieutenant-General Albert C. Wedemeyer after General Stilwell's departure, trained, stiffened and greatly aided the Chinese troops. By the summer of 1945, perhaps 15 to 20 Chinese divisions were equipped with all types of arms up to and including artillery, though not with tanks, and an equal or greater number were partially equipped.[v] The Chinese-American composite wings of the Air Force, largely manned by Chinese trained in the United States, were also functioning well. Meanwhile, American air power in China was being reorganized and strengthened, though the old veteran, Major-General Claire L. Chennault, resigned just before the end. Until the summer of 1945, most of the battle "victories" won in China were actually the result of deliberate Japanese withdrawals. Only then did our prodigious efforts to supply China commence to bring their reward. But the full reward was not to be reaped.

IV

Such was the general situation in the Pacific when the representatives of the three Great Powers met at Potsdam toward the middle of July. The carrier strikes and air assaults had revealed Japan's great air and naval weaknesses. Strategically, she knew that far, far worse was yet to come, as our air power slowly switched its major attention to her land communications and prepared the way for invasion. She had already indicated her awareness that the struggle was hopeless by approaching Soviet Russia in June and, in effect, asking her to mediate. This move came to nothing. The Potsdam Conference opened with Japan strategically defeated but still capable of prolonged resistance (particularly by her land forces) and still able to inflict heavy casualties upon us.

At the Teheran Conference, Marshal Stalin, questioned by President Roosevelt, had indicated his intention of entering the Pacific war. At Yalta, President Roosevelt had raised the question again, and Stalin had agreed (though probably not in writing) to enter the Pacific war either "within" or "about" (the exact phrasing is not known publicly) three months after V-E Day. Stalin is said to have wanted this interval for the redeployment of 30 divisions and their supplies [vi] from Europe to Siberia; certainly three months was a minimum for the proper handling of the major supply problem this would have involved.

Much of the first part of the Potsdam Conference was occupied by a discussion of the Pacific war and the question of Russia's potential entry into it. President Truman, following his predecessor's policies, pressed Russia to set a definite date. Probably he hoped that Russia would sign the Potsdam Declaration, subsequently signed by Britain, China and the United States, outlining the acceptable terms for Japan's surrender. In this observer's opinion, it was a major diplomatic mistake to have stuck to the policies adopted in this connection at Teheran and Yalta. The circumstances at the time of the Potsdam Conference were entirely different. The war against Japan had been strategically won, and it was certain that Russia would enter it without urging on our part. We should have refrained from asking her to come into the Pacific war, simply showing that we considered the decision hers to make, in the light of her own interests.

In any case, Premier Stalin declined to declare war on Japan during the Potsdam Conference. Just prior to Potsdam he had been consulting with Premier Soong of China about Russian-Chinese problems, and he made clear that he wished another meeting with Soong before beginning operations. Tentatively, he set August 15 as the date for the Soviet entry into the war in the Far East. While these deliberations were in progress the great strike of our Third Fleet against Japan began. The tempo of the B-29 attacks was stepped up. Presently – something new in warfare – General LeMay announced to the enemy the names of their cities which would be bombed forthwith.

In the midst of these developments, President Truman received word of the successful test of our first atomic fission bomb experiment in the New Mexico desert – the product of years of combined scientific effort of several nations and of the expenditure of two billion dollars. Apparently he realized the full significance of this event, for the intense effort to persuade the Soviets to declare war quickly was then abandoned. Stalin was told that we had developed a new and terrific explosive; but he seems at first not to have comprehended the import of the disclosure. The Potsdam Declaration, outlining the meaning of unconditional surrender for Japan, was then published, without Stalin's signature.

On August 6, while President Truman was on his way back to the United States, the first atomic fission bomb was dropped on Hiroshima, Japan. On August 8, exactly three months after V-E Day, but one week before the date set at Potsdam, Russia entered the war. On August 9, a second atomic bomb was dropped on Nagasaki. On August 10, Japan indicated her willingness to accept the terms of the Potsdam Declaration. The exact degree of destruction wrought by the atomic bombs can be determined only by inspection on the spot.[vii] Probably, however, most of both cities was destroyed. The effect on morale was of course tremendous, and Russia's declaration of war compounded it. The hopelessness of Japan's position was now even more painfully obvious to the Japanese Government.

There followed a period of limited operations and exchanges of messages. On August 14, United States time (August 15, Japanese time), the United States and British Governments announced that Japan had accepted the Potsdam terms, with the understanding that the Emperor would be left on the throne, though subordinate to the orders of the Allied commander-in-chief of the forces of occupation. General Douglas MacArthur was appointed commander-in-chief for the Allied Nations to receive the surrender and to direct the occupying forces. In the following period our first occupation forces entered Japan and surrender terms were arranged. These finally were signed on September 2 aboard the battleship Missouri in Tokyo Bay. Admiral of the Fleet Chester W. Nimitz signed for the United States....

... Japan's surrender marked probably the first time in history that a great nation had capitulated before an invading soldier had set foot upon her home soil. As a matter of fact, however, our plans for the actual invasion were well advanced and were being pressed to completion. Our "target date" for the invasion of Kyushu was November 1, and the Tokyo plain area was to be invaded March 1, 1946 (though of course these dates were subject to postponement of a few weeks in case of supply difficulties). Japan's unexpectedly quick collapse saved many lives. But the continuing belligerent actions and unrepentant declarations of the Japanese continued after August 10 and were a cause for much disquiet. Some observers felt that, from the political and psychological points of view, the war had ended too soon. The bulk of the Japanese Army was still unbeaten; the Potsdam terms accorded Japan a "softer" peace than we had given Germany; and we had temporized with the Emperor, the fountainhead of the whole militaristic-feudalistic system in Japan. The enemy made it clear in the interval between August 10 and final surrender that he was doing his best to perpetuate that system, and that even though this war had been lost he had hopes for a comeback and was resolved to try to make it. If we allow this trend to continue after we enter Japan, we shall have saved some lives now only to spend more lives later in another war in the Pacific.

The introduction of the atomic bomb dwarfs in importance even the end of almost six years of global warfare. We have entered a new technological age. The harnessing of atomic energy carries implications too vast to be comprehended fully as yet, or to be discussed as yet in detail. Suffice it to say that, strategically and militarily, as well as economically and politically, the world we live in has changed fundamentally.

The greatest war in which the United States ever fought came to an end as suddenly as it began, and with stunning surprise. It had cost us over a million casualties – dead, missing and wounded – and 300 billion dollars in money. But it left the United States incomparably the world's most powerful nation – with or without the atomic bomb. Upon American shoulders lies the terrible responsibility of that power.... [Full Article]

HANSON W. BALDWIN, military and naval correspondent of the New York Times; author of "The Caissons Roll," "Strategy for Victory" and other works

© Foreign Affairs

January 1946

America at War: The Triumph of the Machine [Excerpt]

Hanson W. Baldwin

US M4 Sherman, equipped with a 75 mm main gun, with infantry walking alongside.

THE Second World War was a war of mass, but not, like the First, of massed manpower; it was a war of massed machines. In view of this, American production and construction, which reached Wellsian proportions, can be said to have been directly responsible for the victory over Germany and Japan.

Such a statement, though true in a strictly military sense, is of course only part of the story. This article, summarizing the record of American industrial production and analyzing the merits and defects of certain of the weapons which it turned out, purports to tell only that part. It deliberately leaves out of account the spiritual imponderables which determine how, and how successfully, material power is used. It does not discuss the political factors responsible for the fact that we fought the Axis nations with powerful allies and not alone, and it makes no attempt to describe the brave and great accomplishments of those allies. Instead, it concentrates on the physical aspects of our own war effort. They need to be stressed, for perhaps the chief military lesson of the ordeal through which we have just passed is that although size of armies is an important element in modern warfare, as the Russian campaigns showed, wars today are not won by "big battalions" but by big industries.

Our industrial potential was the greatest advantage which we possessed over our enemies in the Second World War. We possessed no such overwhelming advantage in training for combat, in will-to-fight, in leadership, in tactics and in the quality of our equipment; indeed, the enemy was often on a par with us, or superior to us, in these respects. But we could build an airfield or a pipeline in a fraction of the time the enemy needed; and we could turn out ten tanks to his one. Our armies were not the largest; but together the United States Army, Navy and Air Force undeniably formed the mightiest fighting force ever assembled in history. Our factories and shipyards, operating with our industrial management, skilled workers, factory superintendents, foremen, cost-accountants and efficiency experts – in short, American capital and labor, united in a free-enterprise system – gave that fighting force the sinews of its strength. If ever the United States forgets that industrial "know-how" is essential to victory in modern war, it will be on the way to becoming a second-class Power....

II

"By any standards," the Mead investigating committee of the United States Senate has reported, "the war production task has been a huge success...... The failures have been in the confusion, the delay, and the waste of effort, matériel, and money. More could have been done, and it could have been done sooner and at much less cost. But this is the counsel of perfection and it is the wisdom of hindsight."

What were some of the practical accomplishments of American factories?

Before 1939, it was an accepted truism that wars are fought with the navies in existence at the moment the conflict begins. Not so on this occasion. During this war, the United States built an incomparably larger navy than was possessed by any nation before it began. This fleet, bigger than all the other fleets of the world combined, isolated Japan.

The Navy's "pipeline," or floating-base system of supply, permitted a continuity of naval operations which five or six years earlier was unimaginable. The Fleet's service forces – humble toilers of the sea – serviced the combatant ships so well that the field of fleet operations can now be considered global; the Navy is tied to its base no longer. Before the war, the maximum practicable limit of fleet operations was considered to be 1,500 to 2,500 miles from base. During the war, our ships thought nothing of remaining away from our most advanced permanent bases, Pearl Harbor or the West

Coast, for months and even years on end. The modern fleet in wartime rarely casts anchor. It is refueled, reprovisioned, reammunitioned at sea; it gets mail and movies at sea; new planes from ferry carriers are flown aboard the fleet carriers; new pilots, spare parts, engines – all of the thousand and one items a fleet needs – are brought by the ships of the service forces to the fleet's operating area and transferred at sea. At an advance base in some island atoll, mobile floating drydocks, floating machine shops, barracks ships, water-distilling ships, supply ships, tankers and a score of other types repair and service damaged vessels and give the fleet a "breather" between operations. The logistical achievements of the naval war in the Pacific defy all comparisons.

American shipyards and factories produced this service force – the 829,000 tons of it built in Navy yards and the 2,813,000 tons turned out for the Navy by the Maritime Commission. The development of the process of supply had to be matched by a comparable development of skill in seamanship; it takes a good seaman, indeed, to bring his ship alongside a broad-beamed tanker in a heavy sea and fuel while underway. Good seamen are made by experience, and many were the ships damaged in such operations while green officers learned the A.B.C.'s of blue water. But ship repair and maintenance facilities, at advanced bases and back on the West Coast, though gorged with large numbers of ships damaged by Kamikaze pilots, were always equal to the task. The American Fleet became the most seagoing fleet in the world, though a great many of the Americans who manned it had never before known salt water. This result could not have been attained, however, without the support of a gigantic industry. A vast industrial establishment is now a sine qua non of modern sea power.

The production of the amphibious fleet of almost 80,000 landing craft and boats forms another epic. Our ability to land and supply great forces over open beaches confounded both the Germans and the Japanese. The craft involved, many of them of "Buck Rogers" design, offered peculiar production problems. They were surmounted with a rapidity which amazed the enemy.

Other examples of the indispensability of American industry to the armed services are the special antisubmarine vessels and equipment which were produced at top speed in order to meet the submarine menace. The number of destroyers, destroyer-escorts and patrol vessels of many types which was built is almost incredible. They were equipped with all sorts of amazing new devices, like the antisubmarine rocket launcher called the "hedgehog."

A basic factor not only in the victory on the seas but also in the world-wide victory on land was obviously the bridge of ships produced for the American Merchant Marine. We were able to build ships far faster than the submarines could sink them, even at the height of the U-boat campaign. The total number of Maritime Commission ships built was 5,425, totaling 53,239,000 tons. The millions of tons of special naval combat and auxiliary and amphibious shipping were additional to this figure. Millions of man-hours also went into the work of converting and repairing ships. There has been nothing in history even remotely approximating this shipbuilding achievement.

Perhaps even more impressive was the record of American aircraft construction. When President Roosevelt in early 1942 called for 60,000 planes, many government officials and observers (including this writer) thought he was making a propaganda gesture and that the goal was excessive, if not impossible of attainment. Yet the nation proceeded to produce 296,601 military and special purpose planes, many of them of new design, and incorporated in its production schedule thousands of modifications and changes each year. In other words, the American factory combined flexibility with mass production. Air power, of course, was absolutely indispensable. Without air superiority, the startling victories of the past two years would have been impossible.

The record of the production of weapons for the ground armies was only slightly less impressive than were the shipbuilding and aircraft construction programs. Almost 87,000 tanks, 2,434,553 trucks, 17,400,000 rifles, carbines and sidearms, 315,000 pieces of field artillery and mortars and 4,200,000 tons of artillery shells gave our ground forces the superiority in mobility and fire power which, as General Marshall rightly pointed out, played such a major rôle in our triumph. With them should be mentioned a staggering variety and number of other items, running all the way from 51,000,000 pairs of shoes to 1,412,506 sulfadiazine tablets. In our ground battles we sometimes enjoyed only a slight superiority in numbers (particularly in the early days in North Africa, in the campaigns in Sicily and Italy, and in some of the battles in western Europe), but due to our tremendous production of ammunition and weapons our superiority in fire power was sometimes immense. And the jeep and the two- and-a-half ton truck, as well as the other automotive vehicles, born in Detroit, were the basis of our strategic as well as our tactical land mobility.

Here, then, are three clear-cut ingredients of victory: tremendous superiority at sea and in the air, and on land a superiority in fire power (sometimes slight, but generally marked) and in mobility. The superiority at sea enabled us to project our strength across the oceans, to outflank the enemy, to choose our places for attack, and to land where the enemy was weak. Once our superiority in the air was established, it aided us immeasurably in all combat operations on land and sea, and correspondingly hampered the enemy. It protected our industrial installations and those of our Allies; and it enabled us to project our striking power into the heart of the enemy's country, reducing his industrial output and hence his fire power and mobility. External and internal blockade by sea power and air power were extremely important in weakening the Axis nations. Our massed artillery fire was a product of the factories of America; and our ability to replace matériel losses quickly intensified our hitting power.... [Full Article]

HANSON W. BALDWIN, military and naval correspondent of the New York Times; author of "The Caissons Roll," "Strategy for Victory" and other works

© Foreign Affairs

January/February 1995

The Atomic Bombings Reconsidered

Barton J. Bernstein

Nuclear testing.

THE QUESTIONS AMERICA SHOULD ASK

Fifty years ago, during a three-day period in August 1945, the United States dropped two atomic bombs on Japan, killing more than 115,000 people and possibly as many as 250,000, and injuring at least another 100,000. In the aftermath of the war, the bombings raised both ethical and historical questions about why and how they were used. Would they have been used on Germany? Why were cities targeted so that so many civilians would be killed? Were there likely alternative ways to end the war speedily and avoid the Allies' scheduled November 1, 1945, invasion of Kyushu?

Such questions often fail to recognize that, before Hiroshima and Nagasaki, the use of the A-bomb did not raise profound moral issues for policymakers. The weapon was conceived in a race with Germany, and it undoubtedly would have been used against

Germany had the bomb been ready much sooner. During the war, the target shifted to Japan. And during World War II's brutal course, civilians in cities had already become targets. The grim Axis bombing record is well known. Masses of noncombatants were also intentionally killed in the later stages of the American air war against Germany; that tactic was developed further in 1945 with the firebombing of Japanese cities. Such mass bombing constituted a transformation of morality, repudiating President Franklin D. Roosevelt's prewar pleas that the warring nations avoid bombing cities to spare civilian lives. Thus, by 1945, American leaders were not seeking to avoid the use of the A-bomb on Japan. But the evidence from current archival research shows that by pursuing alternative tactics instead, they probably could still have obviated the dreaded invasion and ended the war by November.

SHIFTING FROM GERMANY TO JAPAN

In 1941, urged by émigré and American scientists, President Roosevelt initiated the atomic bomb project – soon codenamed the Manhattan Project – amid what was believed to be a desperate race with Hitler's Germany for the bomb. At the beginning, Roosevelt and his chief aides assumed that the A-bomb was a legitimate weapon that would be used first against Nazi Germany. They also decided that the bomb project should be kept secret from the Soviet Union, even after the Soviets became a wartime ally, because the bomb might well give the United States future leverage against the Soviets.

By mid-1944, the landscape of the war had changed. Roosevelt and his top advisers knew that the likely target would now be Japan, for the war with Germany would undoubtedly end well before the A-bomb was expected to be ready, around the spring of 1945. In a secret September 1944 memorandum at Hyde Park, Roosevelt and British Prime Minister Winston Churchill ratified the shift from Germany to Japan. Their phrasing suggested that, for the moment anyway, they might have had some slight doubts about actually using the bomb, for they agreed that "it might perhaps, after mature consideration, be used against the Japanese" (my emphasis).

Four days later, mulling over matters aloud with a visiting British diplomat and chief U.S. science adviser Vannevar Bush, Roosevelt briefly wondered whether the A-bomb should be dropped on Japan or whether it should be demonstrated in America, presumably with Japanese observers, and then used as a threat. His speculative notion seemed so unimportant and so contrary to the project's long-standing operating assumptions that Bush actually forgot about it when he prepared a memo of the meeting. He only recalled the president's remarks a day later and then added a brief paragraph to another memorandum.

Put in context alongside the dominant assumption that the bomb would be used against the enemy, the significance of F.D.R.'s occasional doubts is precisely that they were so occasional – expressed twice in almost four years. All of F.D.R.'s advisers who knew about the bomb always unquestioningly assumed that it would be used. Indeed, their memoranda frequently spoke of "after it is used" or "when it is used," and never "if it is used." By about mid-1944, most had comfortably concluded that the target would be Japan.

The bomb's assumed legitimacy as a war weapon was ratified bureaucratically in September 1944 when General Leslie Groves, the director of the Manhattan Project, had the air force create a special group – the 509th Composite Group with 1,750 men – to begin practicing to drop atomic bombs. So dominant was the assumption that the bomb would be used against Japan that only one high-ranking Washington official, Undersecretary of War Robert Patterson, even questioned this notion after V-E Day. He wondered whether the defeat of Germany on May 8, 1945, might alter the plans for dropping the bomb on Japan. It would not.

THE ASSUMPTION OF USE

The Manhattan Project, costing nearly $2 billion, had been kept secret from most cabinet members and nearly all of Congress. Secretary of War Henry L. Stimson, a trusted Republican, and General George C. Marshall, the equally respected army chief of staff, disclosed the project to only a few congressional leaders. They smuggled the necessary appropriations into the War Department budget without the knowledge – much less the scrutiny – of most congressmen, including most members of the key appropriations committees. A conception of the national interest agreed upon by a few men from the executive and legislative branches had revised the normal appropriations process.

In March 1944, when a Democratic senator heading a special investigating committee wanted to pry into this expensive project, Stimson peevishly described him in his diary as "a nuisance and pretty untrustworthy ... He talks smoothly but acts meanly." That man was Senator Harry S Truman. Marshall persuaded him not to investigate the project, and thus Truman did not learn any more than that it involved a new weapon until he was suddenly thrust into the presidency on April 12, 1945.

In early 1945, James F. Byrnes, then F.D.R.'s "assistant president" for domestic affairs and a savvy Democratic politician, began to suspect that the Manhattan Project was a boondoggle. "If [it] proves a failure," he warned Roosevelt, "it will be subjected to relentless investigation and criticism." Byrnes' doubts were soon overcome by Stimson and Marshall. A secret War Department report, with some hyperbole, summarized the situation: "If the project succeeds, there won't be any investigation. If it doesn't, they won't investigate anything else."

Had Roosevelt lived, such lurking political pressures might have powerfully confirmed his intention to use the weapon on the enemy – an assumption he had already made. How else could he have justified spending roughly $2 billion, diverting scarce materials from other war enterprises that might have been even more useful, and bypassing Congress? In a nation still unprepared to trust scientists, the Manhattan Project could have seemed a gigantic waste if its value were not dramatically demonstrated by the use of the atomic bomb.

Truman, inheriting the project and trusting both Marshall and Stimson, would be even more vulnerable to such political pressures. And, like F.D.R., the new president easily assumed that the bomb should and would be used. Truman never questioned that assumption. Bureaucratic developments set in motion before he entered the White House reinforced his belief. And his aides, many inherited from the Roosevelt administration, shared the same faith.

PICKING TARGETS

Groves, eager to retain control of the atomic project, received Marshall's permission in early spring 1945 to select targets for the new weapon. Groves and his associates had long recognized that they were considering a weapon of a new magnitude, possibly equivalent to the "normal bombs carried by [at least] 2,500 bombers." And they had come to assume that the A-bomb would be "detonated well above ground, relying primarily on blast effect to do material damage, [so that even with] minimum probable efficiency, there will be the maximum number of structures (dwellings and factories) damaged beyond repair."

On April 27, the Target Committee, composed of Groves, army air force men like General Lauris Norstad, and scientists including the great mathematician John Von Neumann, met for the first time to discuss how and where in Japan to drop the bomb. They did not want to risk wasting the precious weapon, and decided that it must be dropped visually and not by radar, despite the poor weather conditions in Japan during the summer, when the bomb would be ready.

Good targets were not plentiful. The air force, they knew, "was systematically bombing out the following cities with the prime purpose ... of not leaving one stone lying on another: Tokyo, Yokohama, Nagoya, Osaka, Kyoto, Kobe, Yawata, and Nagasaki ... The air force is operating primarily to laying [sic] waste all the main Japanese cities ... Their existing procedure is to bomb the hell out of Tokyo."

By early 1945, World War II – especially in the Pacific – had become virtually total war. The firebombing of Dresden had helped set a precedent for the U.S. air force, supported by the American people, to intentionally kill mass numbers of Japanese citizens. The earlier moral insistence on noncombatant immunity crumbled during the savage war. In Tokyo, during March 9-10, a U.S. air attack killed about 80,000 Japanese civilians. American B-29s dropped napalm on the city's heavily populated areas to produce uncontrollable firestorms. It may even have been easier to conduct this new warfare outside Europe and against Japan because its people seemed like "yellow subhumans" to many rank-and-file American citizens and many of their leaders.

In this new moral context, with mass killings of an enemy's civilians even seeming desirable, the committee agreed to choose "large urban areas of not less than three miles in diameter existing in the larger populated areas" as A-bomb targets. The April 27 discussion focused on four cities: Hiroshima, which, as "the largest untouched target not on the 21st Bomber Command priority list," warranted serious consideration; Yawata, known for its steel industry; Yokohama; and Tokyo, "a possibility [though] now practically all bombed and burned out and ... practically rubble with only the palace grounds left standing." They decided that other areas warranted more consideration: Tokyo Bay, Kawasaki, Yokohoma, Nagoya, Osaka, Kobe, Kyoto, Hiroshima, Kure, Yawata, Kokura, Shimonoseki, Yamaguchi, Kumamoto, Fukuoka, Nagasaki, and Sasebo.

The choice of targets would depend partly on how the bomb would do its deadly work – the balance of blast, heat, and radiation. At their second set of meetings, during May 11-12, physicist J. Robert Oppenheimer, director of the Los Alamos laboratory, stressed that the bomb material itself was lethal enough for perhaps a billion deadly doses and that the weapon would give off lethal radioactivity. The bomb, set to explode in the air, would deposit "a large fraction of either the initial active material or the radioactive products in the immediate vicinity of the target; but the radiation ... will, of course, have an effect on exposed personnel in the target area." It was unclear, he acknowledged, what would happen to most of the radioactive material: it could stay for hours as a cloud above the place of detonation or, if the bomb exploded during rain or in high humidity and thus caused rain, "most of the active material will be brought down in the vicinity of the target area." Oppenheimer's report left unclear whether a substantial proportion or only a small fraction of the population might die from radiation. So far as the skimpy records reveal, no member of the Target Committee chose to dwell on this matter. They probably assumed that the bomb blast would claim most of its victims before the radiation could do its deadly work.

In considering targets, they discussed the possibility of bombing the emperor's palace in Tokyo and "agreed that we should not recommend it but that any action for this bombing should come from authorities on military policy." They decided to gather information on the effectiveness of using the bomb on the palace.

The Target Committee selected their four top targets: Kyoto, Hiroshima, Yokohama, and Kokura Arsenal, with the implication that Niigata, a city farther away from the air force 509th group's Tinian base, might be held in reserve as a fifth. Kyoto, the ancient former capital and shrine city, with a population of about a million, was the most attractive target to the committee. "From the psychological point of view," the committee minutes note, "there is the advantage that Kyoto is an intellectual center for Japan and [thus] the people there are more apt to appreciate the significance of such a weapon." The implication was that those in Kyoto who survived the A-bombing and saw the horror would be believed elsewhere in Japan.

Of central importance, the group stressed that the bomb should be used as a terror weapon – to produce "the greatest psychological effect against Japan" and to make the world, and the U.S.S.R. in particular, aware that America possessed this new power. The death and destruction would not only intimidate the surviving Japanese into pushing for surrender, but, as a bonus, cow other nations, notably the Soviet Union. In short, America could speed the ending of the war and by the same act help shape the postwar world.

By the committee's third meeting, two weeks later, on May 28, they had pinned down matters. They chose as their targets (in order) Kyoto, Hiroshima, and Niigata, and decided to aim for the center of each city. They agreed that aiming for industrial areas would be a mistake because such targets were small, spread on the cities' fringes, and quite dispersed. They also knew that bombing was imprecise enough that the bomb might easily miss its mark by a fifth of a mile, and they wanted to be sure that the weapon would show its power and not be wasted.

The committee understood that the three target cities would be removed from the air force's regular target list, reserving them for the A-bomb. But, the members were informed, "with the current and prospective rate of ... bombings, it is expected to complete strategic bombing of Japan by 1 Jan 46 so availability of future [A-bomb] targets will be a problem." In short, Japan was being bombed out.

THE RATIFICATION OF TERROR BOMBING

On May 28, 1945, physicist Arthur H. Compton, a Nobel laureate and member of a special scientific panel advising the high-level Interim Committee newly appointed to recommend policy about the bomb, raised profound moral and political questions about how the atomic bomb would be used. "It introduces the question of mass slaughter, really for the first time in history," he wrote. "It carries with it the question of possible radioactive poison over the area bombed. Essentially, the question of the use ... of the new weapon carries much more serious implications than the introduction of poison gas."

Compton's concern received some independent support from General Marshall, who told Secretary Stimson on May 29 that the A-bomb should first be used not against civilians but against military installations – perhaps a naval base – and then possibly against large manufacturing areas after the civilians had received ample warnings to flee. Marshall feared "the opprobrium which might follow from an ill considered employment of such force." A graduate of Virginia Military Institute and a trained soldier, Marshall struggled to retain the older code of not intentionally killing civilians. The concerns of Compton the scientist and Marshall the general, their values so rooted in an earlier conception of war that sought to spare noncombatants, soon gave way to the sense of exigency, the desire to use the bomb on people, and the unwillingness or inability of anyone near the top in Washington to plead forcefully for maintaining this older morality.

The Atomic Bombings Reconsidered

On May 31, 1945, the Interim Committee, composed of Stimson, Bush, Harvard President James Conant, physicist and educator Karl T. Compton, Secretary of State designate James F. Byrnes, and a few other notables, discussed the A-bomb. Opening this meeting, Stimson, the aged secretary of war who had agonized over the recent shift toward mass bombing of civilians, described the atomic bomb as representing "a new relationship of man to the universe. This discovery might be compared to the discoveries of the Copernican theory and the laws of gravity, but far more important than these in its effects on the lives of men."

Meeting, as they were, some six weeks before the first nuclear test at Alamogordo, they were still unsure of the power of this new weapon. Oppenheimer told the group that it would have an explosive force of between 2,000 and 20,000 tons of TNT. Its visual effect would be tremendous. "It would be accompanied by a brilliant luminescence which would rise to a height of 10,000 to 20,000 feet," Oppenheimer reported. "The neutron effect [radiation] would be dangerous to life for a radius of at least two-thirds of a mile." He estimated that 20,000 Japanese would be killed.

According to the committee minutes, the group discussed "various types of targets and the effects to be produced." Stimson "expressed the conclusion, on which there was general agreement, that we could not give the Japanese any warning; that we could not concentrate on a civilian area; but that we should seek to make a profound psychological impression on as many of the inhabitants as possible. At the suggestion of Dr. Conant, the secretary agreed that the most desirable target would be a vital war plant employing a large number of workers and closely surrounded by workers' houses."

Directed by Stimson, the committee was actually endorsing terror bombing – but somewhat uneasily. They would not focus exclusively on a military target (the older morality), as Marshall had recently proposed, nor fully on civilians (the emerging morality). They managed to achieve their purpose – terror bombing – without bluntly acknowledging it to themselves. All knew that families – women, children, and, even in the daytime, during the bomb attack, some workers – dwelled in "workers' houses."

At the committee's morning or afternoon session, or at lunch, or possibly at all three times – different members later presented differing recollections – the notion of a noncombat demonstration of the A-bomb came up. The issue of how to use the bomb was not even on Stimson's agenda, nor was it part of the formal mandate of the Interim Committee, but he may have showed passing interest in the subject of a noncombat demonstration. They soon rejected it. It was deemed too risky for various reasons: the bomb might not work, the Japanese air force might interfere with the bomber, the A-bomb might not adequately impress the Japanese militarists, or the bomb might incinerate any Allied pows whom the Japanese might place in the area.

The discussion on May 31 had focused substantially on how to use the bomb against Japan. At one point some of the members had considered trying several

A-bomb strikes at the same time and presumably on the same city. Groves opposed this notion, partly on the grounds that "the effect would not be sufficiently distinct from our regular air force bombing program." Like the others, he was counting on the dramatic effect of a single bomb, delivered by a single plane, killing many thousands. It was not new for the air force to kill so many Japanese, but this method would be new. And the use of the new weapon would carry, as stressed by American proclamations in early August, the likelihood of more nuclear attacks on Japanese cities – a continuing "rain of ruin."

Two weeks after the Interim Committee meeting, on June 16, after émigré physicists James Franck and Leo Szilard and some colleagues from the Manhattan Project's Chicago laboratory raised moral and political questions about the surprise use of the bomb on Japan, a special four-member scientific advisory committee disposed of the matter of a noncombat demonstration. The group was composed of physicists Arthur Compton, J. Robert Oppenheimer, Enrico Fermi, and Ernest O. Lawrence. By one report, Lawrence was the last of the four to give up hope for a noncombat demonstration. Oppenheimer, who spoke on the issue in 1954 and was not then controverted by the other three men, recalled that the subject of a noncombat demonstration was not the most important matter dealt with during the group's busy weekend meeting and thus did not receive much attention. On June 16, the four scientists concluded: "We can propose no technical demonstration likely to bring an end to the war; we see no acceptable alternative to direct military use."

At that time, as some members of the scientific panel later grudgingly acknowledged, they knew little about the situation in Japan, the power of the militarists there, the timid efforts by the peace forces there to move toward a settlement, the date of the likely American invasion of Kyushu, and the power of the still untested A-bomb. "We didn't know beans about the military situation," Oppenheimer later remarked pungently.

But even different counsel by the scientific advisers probably could not have reversed the course of events. The bomb had been devised to be used, the project cost about $2 billion, and Truman and Byrnes, the president's key political aide, had no desire to avoid its use. Nor did Stimson. They even had additional reasons for wanting to use it: the bomb might also intimidate the Soviets and render them tractable in the postwar period.

Stimson emphasized this theme in a secret memorandum to Truman on April 25: "If the problem of the proper use of this weapon can be solved, we should then have the opportunity to bring the world into a pattern in which the peace of the world and our civilization can be saved." Concern about the bomb and its relationship to the Soviet Union dominated Stimson's thinking in the spring and summer of 1945. And Truman and Byrnes, perhaps partly under Stimson's tutelage, came to stress the same hopes for the bomb.

THE AGONIES OF KILLING CIVILIANS

During 1945, Stimson found himself presiding, with agony, over an air force that killed hundreds of thousands of Japanese civilians. Usually, he preferred not to face these ugly facts, but sought refuge in the notion that the air force was actually engaged in precision bombing and that somehow this precision bombing was going awry. Caught between an older morality that opposed the intentional killing of noncombatants and a newer one that stressed virtually total war, Stimson could neither fully face the facts nor fully escape them. He was not a hypocrite but a man trapped in ambivalence.

Stimson discussed the problem with Truman on June 6. Stimson stressed that he was worried about the air force's mass bombing, but that it was hard to restrict it. In his diary, Stimson recorded: "I told him I was anxious about this feature of the war for two reasons: first, because I did not want to have the United States get the reputation of outdoing Hitler in atrocities; and second, I was a little fearful that before we could get ready the air force might have Japan so thoroughly bombed out that the new weapon would not have a fair background to show its strength." According to Stimson, Truman "laughed and said he understood."

Unable to reestablish the old morality and wanting the benefits for America of the new, Stimson proved decisive – even obdurate – on a comparatively small matter: removing Kyoto from Groves' target list of cities. It was not that Stimson was trying to save Kyoto's citizens; rather, he was seeking to save its relics, lest the Japanese become embittered and later side with the Soviets. As Stimson explained in his diary entry of July 24: "The bitterness which would be caused by such a wanton act might make it impossible during the long post-war period to reconcile the Japanese to us in that area rather than to the Russians. It might thus ... be the means of preventing what our policy demanded, namely, a sympathetic Japan to the United States in case there should be any aggression by Russia in Manchuria."

Truman, backing Stimson on this matter, insisted privately that the A-bombs would be used only on military targets. Apparently the president wished not to recognize the inevitable – that a weapon of such great power would necessarily kill many civilians. At Potsdam on July 25, Truman received glowing reports of the vast destruction achieved by the Alamogordo blast and lavishly recorded the details in his diary: a crater of 1,200 feet in diameter, a steel tower destroyed a half mile away, men knocked over six miles away. "We have discovered," he wrote in his diary, "the most terrible bomb in the history of the world. It may be the fire destruction prophesied." But when he approved the final list of A-bomb targets, with Nagasaki and Kokura substituted for Kyoto, he could write in his diary, "I have told Sec. of War ... Stimson to use it so that military objectives and soldiers and sailors are the target and not women and children. Even if the Japs are savages, ruthless, merciless, and fanatic ... [t]he target will be a purely military one." Truman may have been engaging in self-deception to make the mass deaths of civilians acceptable.

Neither Hiroshima nor Nagasaki was a "purely military" target, but the official press releases, cast well before the atomic bombings, glided over this matter. Hiroshima, for example, was described simply as "an important Japanese army base." The press releases were drafted by men who knew that those cities had been chosen partly to dramatize the killing of noncombatants.

On August 10, the day after the Nagasaki bombing, when Truman realized the magnitude of the mass killing and the Japanese offered a conditional surrender requiring continuation of the emperor, the president told his cabinet that he did not want to kill any more women and children. Rejecting demands to drop more atomic bombs on Japan, he hoped not to use them again. After two atomic bombings, the horror of mass death had forcefully hit the president, and he was willing to return partway to the older morality – civilians might be protected from A-bombs. But he continued to sanction the heavy conventional bombing of Japan's cities, with the deadly toll that napalm, incendiaries, and other bombs produced. Between August 10 and August 14 – the war's last day, on which about 1,000 American planes bombed Japanese cities, some delivering their deadly cargo after Japan announced its surrender – the United States probably killed more than 15,000 Japanese.

THE ROADS NOT TAKEN

Before August 10, Truman and his associates had not sought to avoid the use of the atomic bomb. As a result, they had easily dismissed the possibility of a noncombat demonstration. Indeed, the post-Hiroshima pleas of Japan's military leaders for a final glorious battle suggest that such a demonstration probably would not have produced a speedy surrender. And American leaders also did not pursue other alternatives: modifying their unconditional surrender demand by guaranteeing the maintenance of the emperor, awaiting the Soviet entry into the war, or simply pursuing heavy conventional bombing of the cities amid the strangling naval blockade.

Truman and Byrnes did not believe that a modification of the unconditional surrender formula would produce a speedy surrender. They thought that guaranteeing to maintain the emperor would prompt an angry backlash from Americans who regarded Hirohito as a war criminal, and feared that this concession might embolden the Japanese militarists to expect more concessions and thus prolong the war. As a result, the president and his secretary of state easily rejected Stimson's pleas for a guarantee of the emperor.

Similarly, most American leaders did not believe that the Soviet entry into the Pacific war would make a decisive difference and greatly speed Japan's surrender. Generally, they believed that the U.S.S.R.'s entry would help end the war – ideally, before the massive invasion of Kyushu. They anticipated Moscow's intervention in mid-August, but the Soviets moved up their schedule to August 8, probably because of the Hiroshima bombing, and the Soviet entry did play an important role in producing Japan's surrender on August 14. Soviet entry without the A-bomb might have produced Japan's surrender before November.

The American aim was to avoid, if possible, the November 1 invasion, which would involve about 767,000 troops, at a possible cost of 31,000 casualties in the first 30 days and a total estimated American death toll of about 25,000. And American leaders certainly wanted to avoid the second part of the invasion plan, an assault on the Tokyo plain, scheduled for around March 1, 1946, with an estimated 15,000-21,000 more Americans dead. In the spring and summer of 1945, no American leader believed – as some later falsely claimed – that they planned to use the A-bomb to save half a million Americans. But, given the patriotic calculus of the time, there was no hesitation about using A-bombs to kill many Japanese in order to save the 25,000-46,000 Americans who might otherwise have died in the invasions. Put bluntly, Japanese life – including civilian life – was cheap, and some American leaders, like many rank-and-file citizens, may well have savored the prospect of punishing the Japanese with the A-bomb.

Truman, Byrnes, and the other leaders did not have to be reminded of the danger of a political backlash in America if they did not use the bomb and the invasions became necessary. Even if they had wished to avoid its use – and they did not – the fear of later public outrage spurred by the weeping parents and loved ones of dead American boys might well have forced American leaders to drop the A-bomb on Japan.

No one in official Washington expected that one or two atomic bombs would end the war quickly. They expected to use at least a third, and probably more. And until the day after Nagasaki, there had never been in their thinking a choice between atomic bombs and conventional bombs, but a selection of both – using mass bombing to compel surrender. Atomic bombs and conventional bombs were viewed as supplements to, not substitutes for, one another. Heavy conventional bombing of Japan's cities would probably have killed hundreds of thousands in the next few months, and might have produced the desired surrender before November 1.

Taken together, some of these alternatives – promising to retain the Japanese monarchy, awaiting the Soviets' entry, and even more conventional bombing – very probably could have ended the war before the dreaded invasion. Still, the evidence – to borrow a phrase from F.D.R. – is somewhat "iffy," and no one who looks at the intransigence of the Japanese militarists should have full confidence in those other strategies. But we may well regret that these alternatives were not pursued and that there was not an effort to avoid the use of the first A-bomb – and certainly the second.

Whatever one thinks about the necessity of the first A-bomb, the second – dropped on Nagasaki on August 9 – was almost certainly unnecessary. It was used because the original order directed the air force to drop bombs "as made ready" and, even after the Hiroshima bombing, no one in Washington anticipated an imminent Japanese surrender. Evidence now available about developments in the Japanese government – most notably the emperor's then-secret decision shortly before the Nagasaki bombing to seek peace – makes it clear that the second bomb could undoubtedly have been avoided. At least 35,000 Japanese and possibly almost twice that number, as well as several thousand Koreans, died unnecessarily in Nagasaki.

Administration leaders did not seek to avoid the use of the A-bomb. They even believed that its military use might produce a powerful bonus: the intimidation of the Soviets, rendering them, as Byrnes said, "more manageable," especially in Eastern Europe. Although that was not the dominant purpose for using the weapon, it certainly was a strong confirming one. Had Truman and his associates, like the dissenting scientists at Chicago, foreseen that the A-bombing of Japan would make the Soviets intransigent rather than tractable, perhaps American leaders would have questioned their decision. But precisely because American leaders expected that the bombings would also compel the Soviet Union to loosen its policy in Eastern Europe, there was no incentive to question their intention to use the atomic bomb. Even if they had, the decision would probably have been the same. In a powerful sense, the atomic bombings represented the implementation of an assumption – one that Truman comfortably inherited from Roosevelt. Hiroshima was an easy decision for Truman.

THE REDEFINITION OF MORALITY

Only years later, as government archives opened, wartime hatreds faded, and sensibilities changed, would Americans begin seriously to question whether the atomic bombings were necessary, desirable, and moral. Building on the postwar memoirs of Admiral William Leahy and General Dwight D. Eisenhower, among others, doubts began to emerge about the use of the atomic bombs against Japan. As the years passed, Americans learned that the bombs, according to high-level American military estimates in June and July 1945, probably could not have saved a half million American lives in the invasions, as Truman sometimes contended after Nagasaki, but would have saved fewer than 50,000. Americans also came slowly to recognize the barbarity of World War II, especially the mass killings by bombing civilians. It was that redefinition of morality that made Hiroshima and Nagasaki possible and ushered in the atomic age in a frightening way.

That redefinition of morality was a product of World War II, which included such barbarities as Germany's systematic murder of six million Jews and Japan's rape of Nanking. While the worst atrocities were perpetrated by the Axis, all the major nation-states sliced away at the moral code – often to the applause of their leaders and citizens alike. By 1945 there were few moral restraints left in what had become virtually a total war. Even F.D.R.'s prewar concern for sparing enemy civilians had fallen by the wayside. In that new moral climate, any nation that had the A-bomb would probably have used it against enemy peoples. British leaders as well as Joseph Stalin endorsed the act. Germany's and Japan's leaders surely would have used it against cities. America was not morally unique – just technologically exceptional. Only it had the bomb, and so only it used it.

To understand this historical context does not require that American citizens or others should approve of it. But it does require that they recognize that pre- and post-Hiroshima dissent was rare in 1945. Indeed, few then asked why the United States used the atomic bomb on Japan. But had the bomb not been used, many more, including numerous outraged American citizens, would have bitterly asked that question of the Truman administration.

In 1945, most Americans shared the feelings that Truman privately expressed a few days after the Hiroshima and Nagasaki bombings when he justified the weapons' use in a letter to the Federal Council of Churches of Christ. "I was greatly disturbed over the unwarranted attack by the Japanese on Pearl Harbor and their murder of our prisoners of war," the president wrote. "The only language they seem to understand is the one we have been using to bombard them. When you have to deal with a beast you have to treat him as a beast."

Barton J. Bernstein is Professor of History at Stanford University and Co-Chair of the International Relations Program and the International Policy Studies Program.

© Foreign Affairs

October 1947

Political Problems of a Coalition [Excerpt]

Turning Points of the War

William L. Langer

WIKIMEDIA COMMONS

Roosevelt signing legislation.

... long before the outbreak of the war in Europe Mr. Roosevelt's ideas had taken definite form and had begun to crystallize into policy. He detested the dictatorships and all that they stood for and he regarded their aggressiveness as at least an ultimate threat to this hemisphere and this country. Although public opinion generally shared his aversion, it was for the most part skeptical about the implications of what was loosely called Fascism. There was a good deal of applause for the President's repeated and sometimes unmeasured castigation of Hitler and his ilk, yet there was almost universal opposition to any specific action by this Government, however mild. The President's advocacy of "methods short of war" received a cold reception and his urgent requests for repeal of the arms embargo were turned down despite his insistence that repeal would strengthen his influence for peace. For all its reprobation of Fascist aggression, the American public in 1939 was disgusted with the rest of the world and was determined not to jeopardize its domestic policies or its peace.

Through the American Foreign Service, the Washington Government was probably more fully and accurately informed about the world situation on the eve of the crisis than was any other government in the world. The President and his advisers were under no illusions about the ultimate objectives of Germany, Italy and Japan, nor did they have exaggerated notions about the ability of Britain and France to resist successfully. Envisaging, as they did, the possibility of a Nazi victory in Europe and an effective combination of the German and Japanese efforts, they appreciated to the full the ultimate danger to Latin America and the United States. Their policy, therefore, was to give all possible support to the democracies, within the limitations of the law and the bounds of public opinion. And so was born the first and most fundamental of American policies connected with the war – the identification of our long-term interests with those of Britain and France and the extension of all possible aid to those countries.

This policy was initiated in a very modest way by facilitating the purchase and manufacture of airplanes in this country. Yet when such aid was accidentally revealed in February 1939, it created such a furor in Congress and in the press that it probably deterred the President from too great insistence on repeal of the arms embargo. Only after the agreement between Hitler and Stalin, and Germany's conquest of Poland, was repeal of the embargo carried through Congress by handsome majorities. Although little public reference was made to the full significance of the repeal, it was well understood that the prime objective of the President was to make munitions and supplies available to the democracies. We may therefore conclude that Congress, in repealing the embargo, reflected a growing willingness on the part of the public to follow the President's lead.

It is common knowledge that during the first winter of war the Allies did not take full advantage of the chance to purchase American supplies. They were costly, and the need of them was not fully appreciated. The period of the "phony war" was brought to an abrupt end by the German invasion of Scandinavia, which sent shivers of apprehension through this country as well as through Britain and France. Then came the spectacular collapse of France. In a matter of weeks the prospects of victory had been completely reversed and Britain herself appeared to be on the verge of invasion and conquest. Along with many others, the President waited from day to day – one might say literally from hour to hour – for news that the German attack on the British Isles had begun. He realized more clearly than most Americans that if Britain went under, our bulwark in the Atlantic would be gone and that before long we might be faced with a war on two ocean fronts.

But even though Mr. Roosevelt expected the invasion of Britain, he stuck at all times to the hope that the British would be able to resist successfully. Faith in British determination enabled him to make the fateful decision to send abroad all available matériel without delay, though it should be added that American opinion was not slow in grasping the magnitude of the danger and in tacitly approving whatever action the President deemed necessary. The famous destroyers-for-bases deal, put over in the dark days of September 1940, evoked remarkably little criticism, partly no doubt because the whole transaction was a masterstroke, as important for our own security as it was for the maintenance of Britain's supply lines.

Looking back, we can now see clearly enough that the summer and early autumn of 1940 were the most critical phase of the whole war and that Hitler came nearer victory then than at any later period. That being so, it can be said with considerable assurance that the decision to give all possible support to Britain in her most dangerous hour was the most important and courageous decision made by the United States Government during the entire war period. Europe was in Hitler's hands, and when we decided to support Britain we knew that we might be putting our money on the wrong horse. But the consequences of Britain's defeat were so ominous that we had to take the chance. No matter how desperate the situation, it was still better for us to throw our weight into the struggle than to abandon the last outpost and await the Nazi advance on this side of the Atlantic. We took a chance on Britain, and we won.

The concluding chapter of the program of aiding the anti-Axis forces was written in the Lend-Lease Act of March 1941, which was precipitated by the inability of the British to continue to pay cash for munitions and supplies. As an operational device the Lend-Lease Act made possible for the first time the extension of unlimited aid not only to Britain but to any government engaged in fighting an aggressor. It was literally the key to victory, opening wide the doors to the American arsenal.

III

No positive decision comparable to these decisions in our European policy was ever taken with relation to the Far Eastern situation. If reckoned from the Japanese invasion of Manchuria, the crisis in Asia antedated the Roosevelt Administration as well as the beginning of aggression by Italy and Germany. In one sense our consistent support of Nationalist China against Japan was the prototype of our program of aid to France and Britain. But our policy in Asia, which promised in the first instance to be the touchstone of our entire attitude toward the growing world crisis, never came into clear focus. Originally, Secretary Stimson had proposed a bold move to check aggression and it is quite conceivable that if his proposal had been accepted not only Japan, but Italy and Germany might have been deterred by collective action. Actually, however, nothing was done to block the realization of the Japanese program, and when the rape of Manchuria was followed by the advance into North China in 1937, the tension in Europe was already so great that it was hardly more feasible for the United States Government to take a strong line than for the British to do so. The President and his advisers from that time on adopted an inconclusive position, reflected in the policy of nonrecognition and buttressed by a program of active though modest support for the Government of Chiang Kai-shek. We had, of course, much more effective weapons in our armory; and, in general, American opinion was more disposed to use them in the Far East than in Europe. But the President and Secretary Hull felt, no doubt correctly, that the United States could not afford to become seriously involved with Japan without thereby encouraging aggression in Europe. Our decision with regard to the Far East, then, was essentially a negative one. We muddled along, objecting and protesting and trying to deter Japan by shrouding our policy in uncertainty until the Japanese themselves cut the Gordian knot at Pearl Harbor.

It has often been argued that if we had proceeded firmly with a policy of economic sanctions for Japan, we might have discredited the Japanese militarists and strengthened the liberal, civilian elements with which some sort of acceptable compromise might have been worked out. But actually there is little if any evidence that the Japanese warlords could have been deterred in their plans, which they regarded as vital to the national interest. The chances are, rather, that a positive policy on our part would have provoked hostilities when we were unprepared for them, and when lack of American support might have meant defeat for Britain in Europe. Viewed in this light, the decision not to join issue in the Far East was perhaps as important as any positive decision we could have come to. The Japanese militarists were left to assume the odium of aggression, while the astonishingly prompt declaration of war by Hitler and Mussolini relieved the Government and the country of a decision which, though it was by that time recognized as inevitable, would nonetheless have been a hard one to arrive at. Had we had our choice, we should probably have elected to stay out of the war for another six months at least. But Pearl Harbor, bad as it was, would have been a greater naval disaster had it come a year or six months earlier; and there were inestimable political advantages to this country in having the ultimate decision to go to war in Asia and in Europe imposed upon it.

IV

... No serious political issue was presented by conquered Poland, Denmark, Norway, Belgium or the Netherlands, all of which had set up governments-in-exile which we could and did recognize. But two-fifths of France remained unoccupied under its own government, a government which indeed had concluded an armistice with the Germans and was of necessity more or less under the domination of Hitler, but which nevertheless pretended to some authority in France and to effective control of the French Empire. The question, difficult in itself, was further complicated by the fact that the Vichy Government, under Pétain, was decidedly authoritarian in character and made no secret of its hostility to the democratic system.

In this instance, as in later cases, the President refused to subordinate what he believed to be the national interest to purely ideological considerations. He and his advisers had considerable respect for Marshal Pétain, but no sympathy whatever for subordinates like Laval and Darlan. The United States Government, like the country, despised the Vichy system and detested the Vichy policy of collaboration with the Nazis, but the national interest seemed to be best served by maintaining contact with the French and using such influence as we had to prevent the full victory of the collaborationist elements. Of course this meant turning a cold shoulder to de Gaulle and the Free French Committee in London (though we recognized and assisted the Free French authorities in those parts of the empire where they exercised effective control), and it probably threw some shadows over our rôle as a leader of democracy against Fascism. The fact remains, however, that in cases like this one cannot have one's cake and eat it.[i]

This same problem of compromise with nondemocratic forces was to dog the American Government all through the war and beyond the term of hostilities. The main job throughout was to defeat the Nazi and Fascist dictators and the Japanese militarists. In order to do this we had to coöperate with those who held the same purpose. Britain was one of the few democratic régimes on either side of the conflict. No real objection was raised to our support of Chiang Kai-shek, though his régime could be described as a democratic one only by courtesy. But of course the greatest problem was offered by Soviet Russia, where the issue was not compromise with reaction but association with Communism.

The relations between the United States and Russia had not improved after the recognition of the Soviet Government in 1933. If anything, they had grown worse as a result of the failure of the U.S.S.R. to live up to its obligations. By 1940 they were about as bad as they could be and the distrust in government circles was exceeded only by the intense aversion to the U.S.S.R. of the American public. The Communist system, detested as a threat to the social order and a ruthless dictatorship, was at that time in even worse repute as the partner of Nazism.

When Hitler launched his assault on the Soviet Union, the President and the country were confronted with the question whether to support the Communist régime in its struggle against the invader. The choice of Government and of the American people was in the affirmative: we would send all possible assistance. In actual fact the United States supplied about 10 percent of the Russian requirements in equipment and munitions, representing crucial items without which the Soviet resistance might have proved futile. Though the decision has certainly provoked much searching of soul in the months since victory was assured, it met with remarkably little criticism at the time. The reason seems to me to be a fairly simple one. At the time the situation of Britain was becoming ever more desperate. The primary question was how the war could be won; and about the only hope of victory seemed to lie in bleeding the Germans white on the plains of Russia. The alternative to aiding Russia was to accept Hitler's oft-renewed peace offers, on the basis of recognizing most of his conquests and giving him a free hand against the U.S.S.R., with the extreme likelihood that he would triumph. And that meant a real and terrible danger of Nazi world conquest. In an explanatory letter to the Pope, President Roosevelt expressed himself quite categorically:[ii]

In my opinion, the fact is that Russia is governed by a dictatorship, as rigid in its manner of being as is the dictatorship in Germany. I believe, however, that this Russian dictatorship is less dangerous to the safety of other nations than is the German form of dictatorship. The only weapon which the Russian dictatorship uses outside of its own borders is Communist propaganda which I, of course, recognize has in the past been utilized for the purpose of breaking down the form of government in other countries, religious belief, et cetera. Germany, however, not only has utilized, but is utilizing, this kind of propaganda as well and has also undertaken the employment of every form of military aggression outside of its borders for the purpose of world conquest by force of arms and by force of propaganda. I believe that the survival of Russia is less dangerous to religion, to the church as such, and to humanity in general than would be the survival of the German form of dictatorship.

In short, the President regarded the Communist dictatorship as the lesser of two evils. But beyond that, as we learn from Mr. Welles' recent book, he at once recognized that understanding and coöperation between Moscow and Washington was one of the indispensable foundations for American foreign policy, and was convinced that a firm agreement with the Soviet Government was essential for future peace. He saw no need to fear Communism if an international organization existed, and believed that if Russia could be given security through such an organization, the Communist régime would gradually accommodate itself to the general society of nations. While the Russian and the American systems would probably never meet, they would approximate to the point where there would no longer be a serious problem of living together.[iii]The President shared an idea common at the time that the cult of world revolution was already receding in the minds of the Soviet leaders and that they were becoming more and more engrossed in purely national problems. And, after all, argued the President, Stalin and his associates could not live forever. It might well be that his successors might adopt a more agreeable line. To all these considerations should probably be added the fact that Russia's strength was underestimated and that there seemed to be reason to suppose that the Soviet régime, even if victorious, would be so seriously weakened as to be dependent on the Allied Powers and therefore well-disposed to any program of international organization and action.

To what extent this line of reasoning was sound can be determined only after the lapse of years. For the short run, however, it soon proved to be mistaken. During the first six months, when the Germans just barely failed to reach Moscow, the Soviets were coöperative in every way and did their best to play to the western gallery by demonstrations of religious concessions and so forth. But as soon as the tide began to turn, and particularly after the victory at Stalingrad, they began to change their tune. From that time on the British and Americans were in a perpetual quandary, and it would hardly be going too far to say that all the political decisions of the later period of the war hinged more or less directly on consideration of the Russian problem.

V

In August 1941, the President and Mr. Churchill met in the waters off Argentia, Newfoundland, for the famous conference which produced the Atlantic Charter, a document comparable to the Fourteen Points of President Wilson, but far less specific in its provisions and more general in its appeal. No doubt the primary purpose of the Charter was to afford a common program for all anti-Axis forces and to mark out the lines of a peace settlement for which men everywhere would be willing to fight. But aside from its propaganda value in the democratic countries, we may, I think, assume that it was drafted with an eye to Russia. If the Soviet Government could be brought to subscribe to the provisions of the Charter against territorial aggrandizement and in favor of self-determination of peoples, in favor of equal access to raw materials and freedom of trade, and in favor of a permanent system of security and disarmament, clearly the Allied governments could look to the future with a greater measure of assurance. The Soviet leaders made no objection: along with the other anti-Axis Governments, they signed the Charter and joined the ranks of the United Nations.

But before long the Kremlin began to take a stronger line. There arose the insistent demand for a second front, in addition to the ever-growing requirements for supplies. For a long time a second front in Europe was militarily impossible and had to be evaded or refused. As a result, however, the Allied Governments were more and more haunted by the possibility that the Soviet Government might find it more advantageous to make a deal with Hitler, an idea which it was obviously in the Soviet interest to circulate. To me it seems that these fears were at all times groundless, for it is difficult to see how any Russian-German pact could have been more than a truce, or how Hitler could possibly have offered Stalin anything to compare to the gains he would make by an Allied victory over Germany. The war gave Russia the chance of centuries to dispose of a chronic menace, and as long as there was even a fair chance of success, the Soviets would have been stupid to accept anything less.

The fact of the matter seems to have been that the Soviet leaders were quite as suspicious of their Allies as we were of them. Whether sincerely or otherwise, they took the line that refusal to open a second front was an indication of unwillingness to crush the Nazi power or permit Communist Russia an unqualified victory. It was this mutual suspicion and constant recrimination more than anything else that lay behind the demand for unconditional surrender as formulated by the Casablanca Conference of January 1943 which, incidentally, Stalin refused to attend.

The primary objective of the President and Mr. Churchill at that conference was to reassure the Bolshevik leaders that there would be no compromise with Hitler and that the Allies would fight on to total victory. Whether or not the unconditional surrender formula had the desired effect in the Kremlin we cannot know, but in any event it was a fateful decision; for even if it served to keep the Russians in line, it undoubtedly made the struggle against Nazi Germany more difficult and more prolonged. Far from scaring the Germans into early surrender, it gave the Nazi propagandists their best argument for a last-ditch resistance. On balance it seems that the demand for unconditional surrender was an unfortunate and costly move, and that it was too high a price to pay for Stalin's peace of mind.

VI

The President, influenced no doubt by the widespread criticism of the Paris peacemakers of 1919, seems to have made up his mind at an early date that after the conclusion of hostilities there should be a "cooling-off period" before the negotiation of the final settlement. Like President Wilson before him, he appears to have thought that international organization should come first and that, through collective action, many problems could be disposed of in a spirit of coöperation. Closely related to these ideas was the decision, arrived at with Mr. Churchill, to subordinate everything to the winning of the war and to avoid all political and territorial issues that might provoke dissension among the anti-Axis forces. Sound though this approach might have been, it necessarily presupposed that all parties would postpone final territorial settlements. Actually, the Soviet Government never showed the slightest intention of doing so, and serious difficulties arose almost at once. Hardly had the German armies been stopped before Moscow than Stalin began to press General Sikorski for a discussion of the eastern frontier of Poland. It was no secret that the Soviets, while fighting on the side of the western Powers, were fully determined to retain all that they had acquired through their partnership with Hitler. Sikorski, and after him Mickolajczyk, firmly refused to sacrifice eastern Poland, insisting that they had no constitutional power to barter with the national heritage. At first both the British and American Governments encouraged their stand, though neither Washington nor London was prepared to make an issue of the matter. But by 1943 the British had already weakened considerably, and by 1944 even the President appears to have reconciled himself to Poland's loss of her eastern territories in return for acquisitions at Germany's expense.

By the beginning of 1945 the Soviet armies were already engulfing the Balkan area. Militarily the Allies could do nothing to influence Soviet policy toward countries like Poland, Rumania, Bulgaria, Jugoslavia, Hungary and even Austria. The remaining possibility was to temper the impending storm by discussion and agreement. The Yalta Conference represented the last, almost desperate effort of the President and Mr. Churchill to hold Stalin to the principles of the Atlantic Charter and to save eastern Europe from Bolshevik domination.

The Yalta Conference, like the preceding meeting at Teheran, concerned itself largely with military matters, in this case with the planning for the final assault on Germany. In reality, of course, the outcome of the war was already assured. The defeat of Germany was merely a matter of time and cost. Neither the western Powers nor the Soviets any longer needed each other to clinch the victory. But the President and his advisers, civilian as well as military, still felt that they needed Russian aid to wind up the

Far Eastern conflict. It may be, as General Deane says, that no one seriously doubted that the Soviets would eventually enter the war against Japan, for Russian interests in the Far East were too extensive and important to permit of Moscow's exclusion from the final settlement. But it was obviously in Russia's interest to postpone action in the Far East till the latest possible moment, which would mean that the United States forces would bear the entire burden of Japan's defeat. For many months efforts had been made to get Stalin to commit himself, but the timing of Russian intervention was still not fully decided when the Yalta conferees assembled.

Rightly or wrongly the President was prepared to pay a substantial price for a definite agreement by Stalin to participate in the Far Eastern war. The great fear of the Americans at the time was that the Japanese, even after their home islands had been conquered, might attempt to continue the struggle with the large armies they still had in Manchuria and China. Although it seems unlikely that the Japanese could have continued effective operations on the Asiatic mainland, the only guarantee against such an eventuality was active intervention by the Soviet Far Eastern armies. In short, the President felt that the United States still needed Russian support and thereby was put at a disadvantage in discussion with Stalin. He felt obliged to pay a price for Russian intervention, only to discover later that the Soviet contribution in the Far East was little more than a victory parade. Our own atomic bomb served our purposes a hundred times better than did the Soviet armies.

The price paid for this concession in the military sphere was the recognition of Russia's unilateral settlement of the Polish frontier problem, attenuated only by Soviet acceptance of the vague and ill-defined principle that representative, democratic governments should be established in Poland and other liberated countries. And that was not all. With respect to the all-important German settlement, the President agreed to the compensation of Poland by the cession of German territory, accepted the Russian program for reparations in a general way, and consented to the zonal occupation of Germany along lines exceedingly favorable to the Russians. As everyone knows, these arrangements touching Germany were the prelude to the current struggle for power in Europe. It would be interesting and instructive to follow them in all their ramifications, but that would lead us beyond the scope of this essay. Before leaving the decisions of the Yalta Conference, however, something must be said of the agreements bearing on the plans for world organization.

These plans, proclaimed in the Atlantic Charter, were dear to the heart of the President and enjoyed almost universal support in the United States, where there was general agreement that our failure to join the League of Nations was a fatal blunder. Secretary Hull, through his arduous journey to the Moscow Conference in October 1943, had succeeded in aligning the Soviet Government with the scheme, and the Dumbarton Oaks Conference of August-October 1944 had produced a preliminary draft for the future United Nations organization. But the Russians had at that time insisted on an all-inclusive veto power for each of the five Great Powers sitting on

Political Problems of a Coalition [Excerpt]

the Council and this question had to be left for decision at the highest level. At Yalta the President induced Stalin to retreat somewhat from his initial position, but the real victory remained with the Soviet leader, for the veto power was retained for all but the less important areas of Council procedure. At the San Francisco Conference the Russians refused to be moved from this position, despite all influence that could be brought to bear and despite the vigorous objections of the minor Powers. The history of the United Nations organization since its inauguration is still so fresh that no detailed consideration of this decision of the Yalta Conference is required.

At the time of the Yalta meeting the President was already a very sick man. It is more than likely that his failing health had much to do with his decisions on that occasion. But with that aspect we need not concern ourselves here. The long and the short of it is that the consequences of Yalta were unfortunate on almost every count and that the conference represented a rather sad closing chapter to a war which, on the whole, was wisely directed and gallantly fought.

One is drawn to the conclusion that the brilliant phase of American policy was the initial one, which was followed by a middle phase of expediency and compromise, and a closing phase during which we tried in vain to adjust to the Russian problem. Though this problem has emerged as the key issue of international relations, it is too cheap and easy now to say that the President and the country were misled in the decision which threw in our lot with the Soviets in the summer of 1941. We can see clearly now that it was a mistake to believe that the Bolsheviks had given up the idea of world revolution. Maybe they persist in the revolutionary struggle as a matter of faith and principle. More likely they regard it as the most effective instrument for eliminating their rivals and possible enemies, for the creation of a world fashioned in the Russian image, a world which the Soviet Union can dominate and in which it can therefore feel safe. Be this as it may, Europe and the world have been freed of the Nazi menace only to be confronted with the specter of Communist control.

The prospect of such an eventuality confronted the British and American Governments six years ago. They elected to support the Soviets because the Nazi danger was immediate and frightful, and it was truly perceived also that past treatment of the Soviet régime was at least partially responsible for the isolation and distrust so characteristic of Moscow. It was reasonable to suppose that after a great common effort the Soviets could be drawn into permanent association with other Powers, that mutual confidence and a feeling of security could be developed. After all, the Russian Government and people had a great internal problem of social betterment. They had a vast territory and immeasurable resources. They had no need to expand at the expense of neighbors and they had no ideas of racial superiority to drive them on. Looked at in these terms the crucial decision of 1941 still seems sound.

The really debatable part of our wartime conduct of foreign relations does not hinge on the original decision to aid Russia, but on the subsequent development of policy toward the Soviet Government. It is impossible to focus this criticism on any one problem or single decision. It was a gradual cumulation of questions, characterized perhaps by two chief errors. First, the President unquestionably overestimated his ability to influence Stalin (though here the "might-have-been" result is forever shrouded in uncertainty by his death), and put excessive hope on the possibility of solving the Russian issue through international organization. Second, both Mr. Roosevelt and Mr. Churchill exaggerated the danger that Russia might quit and make a new deal with Hitler. I find it impossible to believe that at any time, as long as there was even a fair chance of victory, it could have been in Stalin's interest to reverse himself. Actually the Soviets were fully as dependent on Allied aid, direct and indirect, as we were on theirs. The idea that during 1942 and 1943 they were carrying the major share of the burden was essentially a mistaken one. Under the circumstances there was no real need for "appeasing" Russia, and certainly no real excuse for acquiescing in Stalin's unilateral action in cases like that of Poland. The idea of sidestepping territorial and other difficult issues may perhaps have been initially sound, but it should not have been adhered to after it had become clear that the Kremlin was exerting its full power to get the settlements it wanted. The United States Government should then have taken a much stronger line. In the case of a showdown, we could have planned much earlier and in a much more constructive way for our own security in western and central Europe. [Full Article]

WILLIAM L. LANGER, Coolidge Professor of Modern History in Harvard University; Chief of Research and Analysis, OSS, 1942-46; author of "The Diplomacy of Imperialism," "Our Vichy Gamble" and other works

© Foreign Affairs

That Was Then: Allen W. Dulles on the Occupation of Germany [Excerpt]

Allen W. Dulles

YEVGENY KHALDEI

Raising a flag over the Reichstag

... THE PRESENT SITUATION IN GERMANY

Digest of a meeting with Allen W. Dulles at the Council on Foreign Relations, December 3, 1945

Germany today is a problem of extraordinary complexity. For two and one-half years the country has been a political and economic void in which discipline was well-maintained. There is no dangerous underground operating there now although some newspapers in the United States played up such a story. The German leaders, of course, could not admit defeat and today the attitude of the people is not so much a feeling of shame and guilt as one of having been let down by their leaders.

Economically and industrially, Germany has scraped the bottom of the barrel, and there are few shops with anything to sell. As soon as you attempt to get Germany to tick and to make arrangements for a government, the lack of men becomes apparent at once. Most men of the caliber required suffer a political taint. When we discover someone whose ability and politics are alike acceptable, we usually find as we did in one case that the man has been living abroad for the past ten years and is hopelessly out of touch with the local situation. We have already found out that you can't run railroads without taking in some Party members.

Labels are always arbitrary and sometimes they effectively mask what lies underneath. For example, citizens A, B, C, and D who didn't care about politics one way or the other were told they had to join the Nazi Party in order to make up the proper quota in the factory in which they worked. The consequences of refusal being what they were, they joined the Party. I know of one instance where two brothers tossed a coin to see which one would join the SS. I mention these things not because I think any substantial number of Germans were opposed to the Party but rather to point out how misleading and decisive a label can be. Furthermore we had altogether too many rules and regulations dealing with the Germans to make an adequate supply of men available to us. There were 126 categories of Germans excluded from any activity or from posts in German administration. Take, for example, the case of a man who owned zinc and coal mines in Upper Silesia. He was a bitter and proven anti-Nazi and a man of undoubted courage and integrity. I was not permitted to use him because he came under category 106, being classified as a war economy supervisor.

We tried hard to find financial advisers, but most of the bankers who had been in Germany in the Twenties and Thirties had by this time been liquidated. I found a banker in the prisoner's cage who had been arrested on an automatic charge because in the early part of the war he had been appointed custodian for the property of an alien, a post he later resigned. I am told that during the period of his responsibility he discharged his trust with scrupulous honesty. I had to bring his case before the Joint Chiefs of Staff in Washington before I was permitted to use him. Then there was Doctor Sauerbruch, one of the leading surgeons in Berlin. Him, also, I found in a cage. It took a cable to London from Washington to get his case straightened out and get him released for useful service, and this had no sooner been done when a few days later the British rearrested him because he came under some other category.

In our zone we arrested 70,000 people. There was no such thing as a habeas corpus and there was no forum to which one could apply for a hearing, although later on we did set up a tribunal of sorts. I do not blame our people too much for this state of affairs. After all, we could not examine each case individually in the early days when the chief task was to occupy Germany in the most effective manner.

That Was Then: Allen W. Dulles on the Occupation of Germany [Excerpt]

The present political set-up in Germany is based on the agreements reached at Tehran, Yalta, and Potsdam. Tehran was made when Churchill felt somewhat shaky. The arrangement did not include the French zone, which was added later. But regardless of its genesis, by and large the scheme is almost entirely unworkable. We have chopped up Baden, Württemburg, and Hesse into artificial zones. In the case of Saxony, the Russian zone cuts off the American and British zones from their counterparts there. It is difficult to see how the Allies could have done otherwise inasmuch as the Russians would not consent to British and American domination of Germany and the Americans and British likewise refused to consider letting Russia get an advantage. Even so, very little progress is being made toward the centralization of the various services. To complicate matters, the French have been saying that they could not set up an administration in the zone assigned to them until they knew what disposition was going to be made of the Rhine and the Ruhr.

In the zone under Russian control the application of Soviet doctrines is thus far confined largely to paper. The Russians are finding it a little difficult to mix collectivist doctrines, including the nationalization of banks, a new system of land tenure, and the creation of a small farmer class, with the set up as it existed under the Nazis and more broadly under a capitalist economy.

We, ourselves, have excellent men on the job. I have the highest regard for Clay, and Eisenhower is a genius as a diplomat and administrator.* Yet I am inclined to think that the problems inherent in the situation are almost too much for us. Our people in Germany are unduly fearful of criticism in the United States. For example, the road between Frankfurt and Wiesbaden is so full of holes that it is almost impossible to drive over it, and one cannot cross the Main between those two places because all the bridges are down. But no repairs are made since the Army feels certain it would be criticized for "restoring the German war potential."

Industry in Germany is at its lowest ebb except for some coal mining in the Ruhr. The minute one considers what industries should be allowed to function and how best to prime the pump in order to set them going, some very real and serious difficulties appear.

So far as the treatment of industry in various zones is concerned, the Russian policy is particularly hard to fathom. It is hard to say whether the Russians really intend to tear down the zone for the purpose of building up Russia, but there is some evidence pointing that way. The Russians have torn up all the double tracks, they are keeping all able-bodied German prisoners, and they have taken East a great many industrialists, bankers, scientists, and the like.

Russian standing in their zone is low. Russian troops are living off the land, and have looted far more than anyone else. They have gone about Berlin looting workers' houses in very much the same way they did in Hungary. This seems to indicate that in both localities the Communist party is not very strong. At any rate, the Russians have seen the West and vice versa.

In the zone being turned over to Poland there is a good deal of buck passing. It is difficult to say what is going on, but in general the Russians are acting little better than thugs. They have wiped out all the liquid assets. No food cards are issued to Germans, who are forced to travel on foot into the Russian zone, often more dead than alive. An iron curtain has descended over the fate of these people and very likely conditions are truly terrible. The promises at Yalta to the contrary, probably 8 to 10 million people are being enslaved. Unquestionably Germany should be punished. In this instance, however, I think there will remain a legacy of bitterness which will not bode well for the future.

I have already said that the problem of Germany very nearly defies a successful solution. The question is: What can we do? The first step is to get together in dealing with what is at bottom a common problem. Next, we must find people we can use. We might use the churches which did not knuckle under to Hitler, although it is questionable in the minds of some people whether churches should get into politics. We might also consider the survivors of the affair of July 20* and see what material the trade unions can furnish. Finally, we can screen the prisoners of war.

The women will not be much help to us, although in theory they could be. A saying now current in Germany is that today most of the able-bodied men are women. Hitler had an enormous hold over them and Eva Braun's existence appeared to be unknown to most of them. They are extremely bitter. Altogether the problem deserves very careful study.

I think it may well become necessary for us to change the form of our occupation. Thus far there has been very little disturbance or misbehavior on the part of our troops. I think we ought to use small, highly mechanized units and put our reliance on planes. These forces I would quarter outside of the cities, lest their presence create a talking point for German propaganda against the occupation.

Trying to arrive at figures in order to set up a standard of living in Germany is a difficult and almost hopeless problem, and one perhaps beyond the ingenuity of man. And yet we must somehow find a solution.

Germany ought to be put to work for the benefit of Europe and particularly for the benefit of those countries plundered by the Nazis. If we do not find some work for the Germans and if we do not solve the refugee problem,* the Germans will have their revenge in one form or another though it takes a hundred years. [Full Article]

... *Editors' note. An unsuccessful 1944 coup attempt by anti-Hitler elements in the German army and military intelligence.

*Editors' note. At the time, Generals Lucius Clay and Dwight Eisenhower were the deputy military governor and military governor of Germany, respectively.

*Editors' note. The country was then flooded with millions of ethnic Germans displaced from territories to the east.

© Foreign Affairs

January 1947

The Nuremberg Trial: Landmark in Law [Excerpt]

Henry L. Stimson

Defendants in the dock. The main target of the prosecution was Hermann Göring (at the left edge on the first row of benches), considered to be the most important surviving official in the Third Reich after Hitler's death.

IN THE confusion and disquiet of the war's first aftermath, there has been at least one great event from which we may properly take hope. The surviving leaders of the Nazi conspiracy against mankind have been indicted, tried, and judged in a proceeding whose magnitude and quality make it a landmark in the history of international law. The great undertaking at Nuremberg can live and grow in meaning, however, only if its principles are rightly understood and accepted. It is therefore disturbing to find that its work is criticized and even challenged as lawless by many who should know better. In the deep conviction that this trial deserves to be known and valued as a long step ahead on the only upward road, I venture to set down my general view of its nature and accomplishment.

The defendants at Nuremberg were leaders of the most highly organized and extensive wickedness in history. It was not a trick of the law which brought them to the bar; it was the "massed angered forces of common humanity." There were three

The Nuremberg Trial: Landmark in Law [Excerpt]

different courses open to us when the Nazi leaders were captured: release, summary punishment, or trial. Release was unthinkable; it would have been taken as an admission that there was here no crime. Summary punishment was widely recommended. It would have satisfied the immediate requirement of the emotions, and in its own roughhewn way it would have been fair enough, for this was precisely the type of justice that the Nazis themselves had so often used. But this fact was in reality the best reason for rejecting such a solution. The whole moral position of the victorious Powers must collapse if their judgments could be enforced only by Nazi methods. Our anger, as righteous anger, must be subject to the law. We therefore took the third course and tried the captive criminals by a judicial proceeding. We gave to the Nazis what they had denied their own opponents – the protection of the Law. The Nuremberg Tribunal was thus in no sense an instrument of vengeance but the reverse. It was, as Mr. Justice Jackson said in opening the case for the prosecution, "one of the most significant tributes that Power has ever paid to Reason."

The function of the law here, as everywhere, has been to insure fair judgment. By preventing abuse and minimizing error, proceedings under law give dignity and method to the ordinary conscience of mankind. For this purpose the law demands three things: that the defendant be charged with a punishable crime; that he have full opportunity for defense; and that he be judged fairly on the evidence by a proper judicial authority. Should it fail to meet any one of these three requirements, a trial would not be justice. Against these standards, therefore, the judgment of Nuremberg must itself be judged....

... A single landmark of justice and honor does not make a world of peace. The Nazi leaders are not the only ones who have renounced and denied the principles of western civilization. They are unique only in the degree and violence of their offenses. In every nation which acquiesced even for a time in their offense, there were offenders. There have been still more culpable offenders in nations which joined before or after in the brutal business of aggression. If we claimed for Nuremberg that it was final justice, or that only these criminals were guilty, we might well be criticized as being swayed by vengeance and not justice. But this is not the claim. The American prosecutor has explicitly stated that he looks uneasily and with great regret upon certain brutalities that have occurred since the ending of the war. He speaks for us all when he says that there has been enough bloodletting in Europe. But the sins of others do not make the Nazi leaders less guilty, and the importance of Nuremberg lies not in any claim that by itself it clears the board, but rather in the pattern it has set. The four nations prosecuting, and the 19 others subscribing to the Charter of the international Military Tribunal, have firmly bound themselves to the principle that aggressive war is a personal and punishable crime.

It is this principle upon which we must henceforth rely for our legal protection against the horrors of war. We must never forget that under modern conditions of life, science and technology, all war has become greatly brutalized, and that no one who joins in it, even in self-defense, can escape becoming also in a measure brutalized. Modern war cannot be limited in its destructive methods and in the inevitable debasement of all participants. A fair scrutiny of the last two World Wars makes clear the steady intensification in the inhumanity of the weapons and methods employed by both the aggressors and the victors. In order to defeat Japanese aggression, we were forced, as Admiral Nimitz has stated, to employ a technique of unrestricted submarine warfare not unlike that which 25 years ago was the proximate cause of our entry into World War I. In the use of strategic air power, the Allies took the lives of hundreds of thousands of civilians in Germany, and in Japan the destruction of civilian life wreaked by our B-29s, even before the final blow of the atomic bombs, was at least proportionately great. It is true that our use of this destructive power, particularly of the atomic bomb, was for the purpose of winning a quick victory over aggressors, so as to minimize the loss of life, not only of our troops but of the civilian populations of our enemies as well, and that this purpose in the case of Japan was clearly effected. But even so, we as well as our enemies have contributed to the proof that the central moral problem is war and not its methods, and that a continuance of war will in all probability end with the destruction of our civilization.

International law is still limited by international politics, and we must not pretend that either can live and grow without the other. But in the judgment of Nuremberg there is affirmed the central principle of peace – that the man who makes or plans to make aggressive war is a criminal. A standard has been raised to which Americans, at least, must repair; for it is only as this standard is accepted, supported and enforced that we can move onward to a world of law and peace. [Full Article]

HENRY L. STIMSON, Secretary of State, 1929-1933; Secretary of War, 1911-1913, and 1940-1945; Chairman of the U. S. Delegation to the London Naval Conference, 1930, and to the Disarmament Conference, 1932

© Foreign Affairs

July 1947

The Sources of Soviet Conduct [Excerpt]

"X" (George F. Kennan)

Soviet tanks face U.S. tanks at Checkpoint Charlie, October 27, 1961

... Soviet pressure against the free institutions of the Western world is something that can be contained by the adroit and vigilant application of counterforce at a series of constantly shifting geographical and political points, corresponding to the shifts and maneuvers of Soviet policy, but which cannot be charmed or talked out of existence. The Russians look forward to a duel of infinite duration, and they see that already they have scored great successes. It must be borne in mind that there was a time when the Communist Party represented far more of a minority in the sphere of Russian national life than Soviet power today represents in the world community.

It is clear that the United States cannot expect in the foreseeable future to enjoy political intimacy with the Soviet regime. It must continue to regard the Soviet Union as a rival, not a partner, in the political arena. It must continue to expect that Soviet policies will reflect no abstract love of peace and stability, no real faith in the possibility of a permanent happy coexistence of the Socialist and capitalist worlds, but rather a cautious, persistent pressure toward the disruption and weakening of all rival influence and rival power.

Balanced against this are the facts that Russia, as opposed to the western world in general, is still by far the weaker party, that Soviet policy is highly flexible, and that Soviet society may well contain deficiencies which will eventually weaken its own total potential. This would of itself warrant the United States entering with reasonable confidence upon a policy of firm containment, designed to confront the Russians with unalterable counterforce at every point where they show signs of encroaching upon the interest of a peaceful and stable world.

But in actuality the possibilities for American policy are by no means limited to holding the line and hoping for the best. It is entirely possible for the United States to influence by its actions the internal developments, both within Russia and throughout the international Communist movement, by which Russian policy is largely determined. This is not only a question of the modest measure of informational activity which this government can conduct in the Soviet Union and elsewhere, although that, too, is important. It is rather a question of the degree to which the United States can create among the peoples of the world generally the impression of a country which knows what it wants, which is coping successfully with the problems of its internal life and with the responsibilities of a world power, and which has a spiritual vitality capable of holding its own among the major ideological currents of the time. To the extent that such an impression can be created and maintained, the aims of Russian Communism must appear sterile and quixotic, the hopes and enthusiasm of Moscow's supporters must wane, and added strain must be imposed on the Kremlin's foreign policies. For the palsied decrepitude of the capitalist world is the keystone of Communist philosophy. Even the failure of the United States to experience the early economic depression which the ravens of the Red Square have been predicting with such complacent confidence since hostilities ceased would have deep and important repercussions throughout the Communist world.

By the same token, exhibitions of indecision, disunity and internal disintegration within this country have an exhilarating effect on the whole Communist movement. At each evidence of these tendencies, a thrill of hope and excitement goes through the Communist world; a new jauntiness can be noted in the Moscow tread; new groups of foreign supporters climb on to what they can only view as the bandwagon of international politics; and Russian pressure increases all along the line in international affairs.

In would be an exaggeration to say that American behavior unassisted and alone could exercise a power of life and death over the Communist movement and bring about the early fall of Soviet power in Russia. But the United States has it in its power

The Sources of Soviet Conduct [Excerpt]

to increase enormously the strains under which Soviet policy must operate, to force upon the Kremlin a far greater degree of moderation and circumspection than it has had to observe in recent years, and in this way to promote tendencies which must eventually find their outlet in either the breakup or the gradual mellowing of Soviet power. For no mystical, messianic movement – and particularly not that of the Kremlin – can face frustration indefinitely without eventually adjusting itself in one way or another to the logic of that state of affairs.... [Full Article]

© Foreign Affairs

October 1948

The Atom Bomb as Policy Maker [Excerpt]

Bernard Brodie

A mockup of the Fat Man nuclear device.

IT IS now three years since an explosion over Hiroshima revealed to the world that man had been given the means of destroying himself. Eight atomic bombs have now been detonated – assuming that the three "atomic weapons" tested at Eniwetok were in fact bombs – and each was in itself a sufficient warning that the promise of eventual benefits resulting from the peacetime use of atomic energy must count as nothing compared to the awful menace of the bomb itself. The good things of earth cannot be enjoyed by dead men, nor can societies which have lost the entire material fabric of their civilization survive as integrated organisms.

Yet the dilemma nevertheless faces us that the enforcement of tolerable behavior among nations will continue for an indefinite time in the future to depend at least occasionally upon coercion or the threat of it, that the instruments of coercion against Great Powers will most likely be found only in the hands of other Great Powers (who can dispense with them only by acknowledging their readiness to forfeit whatever liberties they may happen blessedly to possess), and that those instruments appear fated, largely because of those same imperfections of our society which make power necessary, to include the atomic bomb and perhaps other comparable instruments of mass destruction.

Individuals may retreat from this dilemma behind a barrage of high moral protestation, usually combined with glowing predictions of a better world to be. Such retreat is rendered doubly sweet because it is more often than not accompanied by applause, especially from the intellectual wing of our society. But the nation as a whole cannot retreat from the problem, and those who desert simply leave the others to think it through as best they can.

The impact of the atomic bomb on United States policy has thus far been evidenced most clearly in the almost frantic effort to secure the adoption of a system of international control of atomic energy. It is difficult if not impossible to find an historical precedent for the eagerness with which this nation has pursued an endeavor which, if successful, would deprive it of the advantages of monopoly possession of a decisive military weapon. To be sure, the monopoly is bound to be temporary, but that has always been true of new weapons, the monopoly possession of which has usually been jealously guarded for as long as possible. The United States is even now behaving in the customary manner concerning all new weapons other than those based on the explosive release of atomic energy, a fact which in itself sufficiently demonstrates that the exceptional American position on atomic energy control is based on something other than national generosity. That "something other" is of course a well-warranted fear of living in a world which morally and politically is little different from the one we have known but which in addition is characterized by multilateral possession of atomic weapons.

But the fear which engendered the pursuit of international control also provoked the resolve that any control scheme must contain within itself practically watertight guarantees against evasion or violation. That was and remains a wholly reasonable resolve, but its inevitable consequence is that it greatly reduces the chance of securing the requisite agreement. Two years of work by the United Nations Atomic Energy Commission have resulted in some illumination of the problem but almost no progress towards a solution. American initiative in securing formal suspension of the activities of the Commission is a plain acknowledgment of that fact.

But where does that leave us? It leaves us, for one thing, with the unwanted bomb still in our hands, and, so far as we know, still exclusively in our hands. It leaves us also under the compulsion to go on building more bombs, and better ones if possible. We must continue our search for a workable and secure international control system by any corridor which reflects even a glimmer of hope of success, but we must also begin to consider somewhat more earnestly and responsibly than we have thus far what it will mean for the nation… [Full Article]

BERNARD BRODIE, member of the Yale Institute of International Studies and Associate Professor of International Relations, Yale University; author of "Sea Power in the Machine Age" and "A Guide to Naval Strategy"

© Foreign Affairs

April 1949

The Illusion of World Government [Excerpt]

Reinhold Niebuhr

Representatives of 26 United Nations attend Flag Day ceremonies in the White House in 1942.

THE trustful acceptance of false solutions for our perplexing problems adds a touch of pathos to the tragedy of our age.

The tragic character of our age is revealed in the world-wide insecurity which is the fate of modern man. Technical achievements, which a previous generation had believed capable of solving every ill to which the human flesh is heir, have created, or at least accentuated, our insecurity. For the growth of technics has given the perennial problems of our common life a more complex form and a scope that has grown to be world-wide.

Our problem is that technics have established a rudimentary world community but have not integrated it organically, morally or politically. They have created a community of mutual dependence, but not one of mutual trust and respect. Without this higher integration, advancing technics tend to sharpen economic rivalries within a general framework of economic interdependence; they change the ocean barriers of yesterday into the battlegrounds of today; and they increase the deadly efficacy of the instruments of war so that vicious circles of mutual fear may end in atomic conflicts and mutual destruction. To these perplexities an ideological conflict has been added, which divides the world into hostile camps.

It is both necessary and laudable that men of good will should, in this situation, seek to strengthen every moral and political force which might give a rudimentary world community a higher degree of integration. It was probably inevitable that the desperate plight of our age should persuade some well meaning men that the gap between a technically integrated and politically divided community could be closed by the simple expedient of establishing a world government through the fiat of the human will and creating world community by the fiat of world government. It is this hope which adds a touch of pathos to already tragic experiences. The hope not only beguiles some men from urgent moral and political responsibilities. It tempts others into irresponsible criticisms of the necessarily minimal constitutional structure which we have embodied in the United Nations and which is as bad as its critics aver only if a better one is within the realm of possibilities.

Virtually all arguments for world government rest upon the simple presupposition that the desirability of world order proves the attainability of world government. Our precarious situation is unfortunately no proof, either of the moral ability of mankind to create a world government by an act of the will, nor of the political ability of such a government to integrate a world community in advance of a more gradual growth of the "social tissue" which every community requires more than government.

Most advocates of world government also assume that nations need merely follow the alleged example of the individuals of another age who are supposed to have achieved community by codifying their agreements into law and by providing an agency of some kind for law enforcement. This assumption ignores the historic fact that the mutual respect for each other's rights in particular communities is older than any code of law; and that machinery for the enforcement of law can be efficacious only when a community as a whole obeys its laws implicitly, so that coercive enforcement may be limited to a recalcitrant minority.

The fallacy of world government can be stated in two simple propositions. The first is that governments are not created by fiat (though sometimes they can be imposed by tyranny). The second is that governments have only limited efficacy in integrating a community....

... In short, the forces which are operating to integrate the world community are limited. To call attention to this fact does not mean that all striving for a higher and wider integration of the world community is vain. That task must and will engage the conscience of mankind for ages to come. But the edifice of government which we build will be sound and useful if its height is proportionate to the strength of the materials from which it is constructed. The immediate political situation requires that we seek not only peace, but also the preservation of a civilization which we hold to be preferable to the universal tyranny with which Soviet aggression threatens us. Success in this double task is the goal; let us not be diverted from it by the pretense that there is a simple alternative.... [Full Article]

REINHOLD NIEBUHR, Professor of Applied Christianity in the Union Theological Seminary, New York; author of many works on philosophical, religious and political subjects, the latest of them "Faith and History"

© Foreign Affairs

May/June 1996

The Myth of Post-Cold War Chaos [Excerpt]

G. John Ikenberry

THIERRY NOIR / WIKIMEDIA COMMONS

The Berlin Wall, 1986.

A great deal of ink has been shed in recent years describing various versions of the post-Cold War order. These attempts have all failed, because there is no such creature. The world order created in the 1940s is still with us, and in many ways stronger than ever. The challenge for American foreign policy is not to imagine and build a new world order but to reclaim and renew an old one – an innovative and durable order that has been hugely successful and largely unheralded.

The end of the Cold War, the common wisdom holds, was a historical watershed. The collapse of communism brought the collapse of the order that took shape after World War II. While foreign policy theorists and officials scramble to design new grand strategies, the United States is rudderless on uncharted seas.

The common wisdom is wrong. What ended with the Cold War was bipolarity, the nuclear stalemate, and decades of containment of the Soviet Union – seemingly the most dramatic and consequential features of the postwar era. But the world order created in the middle to late 1940s endures, more extensive and in some respects more robust than during its Cold War years. Its basic principles, which deal with organization and relations among the Western liberal democracies, are alive and well.

These less celebrated, less heroic, but more fundamental principles and policies – the real international order – include the commitment to an open world economy and its multilateral management, and the stabilization of socioeconomic welfare. And the political vision behind the order was as important as the anticipated economic gains. The major industrial democracies took it upon themselves to "domesticate" their dealings through a dense web of multilateral institutions, intergovernmental relations, and joint management of the Western and world political economies....

World War II produced two postwar settlements. One, a reaction to deteriorating relations with the Soviet Union, led to the containment order, which was based on the balance of power, nuclear deterrence, and political and ideological competition. The other, a reaction to the economic rivalry and political turmoil of the 1930s and the resulting world war, can be called the liberal democratic order. It culminated in a wide range of new institutions and relations among the Western industrial democracies, built around economic openness, political reciprocity, and multilateral management of an American-led liberal political system....

... The liberal democratic agenda was less obviously a grand strategy designed to advance American security interests [than was containment], and it was inevitably viewed during the Cold War as secondary, a preoccupation of economists and businessmen. The policies and institutions that supported free trade among the advanced industrial societies seemed the stuff of low politics. But the liberal democratic agenda was actually built on a robust yet sophisticated set of ideas about American security interests, the causes of war and depression, and a desirable postwar political order....

The most basic conviction underlying the postwar liberal agenda was that the closed autarkic regions that had contributed to the worldwide depression and split the globe into competing blocs before the war must be broken up and replaced by an open, nondiscriminatory economic system. Peace and security, proponents had decided, were impossible in the face of exclusive economic regions. The challengers of liberal multilateralism, however, occupied almost every corner of the advanced industrial world. Germany and Japan were the most overtly hostile; both had pursued a dangerous path that combined authoritarian capitalism with military dictatorship and coercive regional autarky. But the British Commonwealth and its imperial preference system also challenged liberal multilateral order.

The hastily drafted Atlantic Charter was an American effort to ensure that Britain signed on to its liberal democratic war aims. The joint statement of principles affirmed free trade, equal access to natural resources for all interested buyers, and international economic collaboration to advance labor standards, employment security, and social welfare. Roosevelt and Churchill declared before the world that they had learned the lessons of the interwar years – and those lessons were fundamentally about the proper organization of the Western political economy. America's enemies, its friends, and even America itself had to be reformed and integrated into the postwar economic system.

The postwar liberal democratic order was designed to solve the internal problems of Western industrial capitalism. It was not intended to fight Soviet communism, nor was it simply a plan to get American business back on its feet after the war by opening up the world to trade and investment. It was a strategy to build Western solidarity through economic openness and joint political governance. Four principles pursued in the 1940s gave shape to this order.

The most obvious principle was economic openness, which would ideally take the form of a system of nondiscriminatory trade and investment.... American thinking was that economic openness was an essential element of a stable and peaceful world political order. "Prosperous neighbors are the best neighbors," remarked Roosevelt administration Treasury official Harry Dexter White. But officials were convinced that American economic and security interests demanded it as well. Great liberal visionaries and hard-nosed geopolitical strategists could agree on the notion of open markets; it united American postwar planners and was the seminal idea informing the work of the Bretton Woods conference on postwar economic cooperation....

The second principle was joint management of the Western political-economic order. The leading industrial democratic states must not only lower barriers to trade and the movement of capital but must govern the system. This also was a lesson from the 1930s: institutions, rules, and active mutual management by governments were necessary to avoid unproductively competitive and conflictual economic practices. Americans believed such cooperation necessary in a world where national economies were increasingly at the mercy of developments abroad. The unwise or untoward policies of one country threatened contagion, undermining the stability of all. As Roosevelt said at the opening of Bretton Woods, "The economic health of every country is a proper matter of concern to all its neighbors, near and far." ...

A third principle of liberal democratic order held that the rules and institutions of the Western world economy must be organized to support domestic economic stability and social security. This new commitment was foreshadowed in the Atlantic Charter's call for postwar international collaboration to ensure employment stability and social welfare. It was a sign of the times that Churchill, a conservative Tory, could promise a historic expansion of the government's responsibility for the people's well-being. In their schemes for postwar economic order, both Britain and the United States sought a system that would aid and protect their nascent social and economic commitments. They wanted an open world economy, but one congenial to the emerging welfare state as well as business.

The discovery of a middle way between old political alternatives was a major innovation of the postwar Western economic order. British and American planners began their discussion in 1942 deadlocked, Britain's desire for full employment and economic stabilization after the war running up against the American desire for free trade. The breakthrough came in 1944 with the Bretton Woods agreements on monetary order, which secured a more or less open system of trade and payments while providing safeguards for domestic economic stability through the International Monetary Fund. The settlement was a synthesis that could attract a new coalition of conservative free traders and the liberal prophets of economic planning.

A final element of the liberal democratic system might be termed "constitutionalism" – meaning simply that the Western nations would make systematic efforts to anchor their joint commitments in principled and binding institutional mechanisms. In fact, this may be the order's most basic aspect, encompassing the other principles and policies and giving the whole its distinctive domestic character. Governments might ordinarily seek to keep their options open, cooperating with other states but retaining the possibility of disengagement. The United States and the other Western nations after the war did exactly the opposite. They built long-term economic, political, and security commitments that were difficult to retract, and locked in the relationships, to the extent that sovereign states can....

For those who thought cooperation among the advanced industrial democracies was driven primarily by Cold War threats, the last few years must appear puzzling. Relations between the major Western countries have not broken down. Germany has not rearmed, nor has Japan. What the Cold War focus misses is an appreciation of the other, less heralded, postwar American project – the building of a liberal order in the West. Archaeologists remove one stratum only to discover an older one beneath; the end of the Cold War allows us to see a deeper and more enduring layer of the postwar political order that was largely obscured by the more dramatic struggles between East and West.

Fifty years after its founding, the Western liberal democratic world is robust, and its principles and policies remain the core of world order. The challenges to liberal multilateralism both from within and from outside the West have mainly disappeared. Although regional experiments abound, they are fundamentally different from the autarkic blocs of the 1930s. The forces of business and financial integration are moving the globe inexorably toward a more tightly interconnected system that ignores regional as well as national borders....

Some aspects of the vision of the 1940s have faded. The optimism about government activism and economic management that animated the New Deal and Keynesianism has been considerably tempered. Likewise, the rule-based, quasi-judicial functions of liberal multilateralism have eroded, particularly in monetary relations. Paradoxically, although the rules of cooperation have become less coherent, cooperation itself has increased. Formal rules governing the Western world economy have gradually been replaced by a convergence of thinking on economic policy. The consensus on the broad outlines of desirable domestic and international economic policies has both reflected and promoted increased economic growth and the incorporation of emerging economies into the system.

The problems the liberal democratic order confronts are mostly problems of success, foremost among them the need to integrate the newly developing and post-communist countries. Here one sees most clearly that the post-Cold War order is really a continuation and extension of the Western order forged during and after World War II. The difference is its increasingly global reach. The world has seen an explosion in the desire of countries and peoples to move toward democracy and capitalism. When the history of the late twentieth century is written, it will be the struggle for more open and democratic polities throughout the world that will mark the era, rather than the failure of communism.

Other challenges to the system are boiling up in its leading states. In its early years, rapid and widely shared economic growth buoyed the system, as working- and middle-class citizens across the advanced industrial world rode the crest of the boom. Today economic globalization is producing much greater inequality between the winners and the losers, the wealthy and the poor. How the subsequent dislocations, dashed expectations, and political grievances are dealt with – whether the benefits are shared and the system as a whole is seen as socially just – will affect the stability of the liberal world order more than regional conflict…. [Full Article]

G. JOHN IKENBERRY is *Co-Director of the Lauder Institute of Management and International Studies and Associate Professor of Political Science at the University of Pennsylvania.*

© Foreign Affairs

www.ingramcontent.com/pod-product-compliance
Lightning Source LLC
Chambersburg PA
CBHW080510110426
42742CB00017B/3057